CUSTOM EDITION

Selected Readings from

Understanding Human Communication

Ronald B. Adler
Santa Barbara City College

George Rodman
Brooklyn College, City University of New York

New York   Oxford
OXFORD UNIVERSITY PRESS
2010

Oxford University Press, Inc., publishes works that further Oxford University's
objective of excellence in research, scholarship, and education.

Oxford   New York
Auckland   Cape Town   Dar es Salaam   Hong Kong   Karachi
Kuala Lumpur   Madrid   Melbourne   Mexico City   Nairobi
New Delhi   Shanghai   Taipei   Toronto

With offices in
Argentina   Austria   Brazil   Chile   Czech Republic   France   Greece
Guatemala   Hungary   Italy   Japan   Poland   Portugal   Singapore
South Korea   Switzerland   Thailand   Turkey   Ukraine   Vietnam

Published by Oxford University Press, Inc.
198 Madison Avenue, New York, New York 10016
http://www.oup.com

ISBN: 978-0-19-977418-0

CHAPTER 1

Human Communication: What and Why

After studying the material in this chapter ...

You should understand:

1. The working definition and characteristics of *communication*.
2. The types of communication covered in this book.
3. The needs satisfied by communication.
4. The characteristics of linear and transactional communication models.
5. The characteristics of competent communication.
6. Common misconceptions about communication.

You should be able to:

1. Define *communication* and give specific examples of the various types of communication introduced in this chapter.
2. Describe the key needs you attempt to satisfy in your life by communicating.
3. Use the criteria in this chapter to identify the degree to which communication (yours or others') in a specific situation is competent and suggest ways of increasing the competence level.
4. Identify how misconceptions about communication can create problems and suggest how a more accurate analysis of the situations you describe can lead to better outcomes.

Communication Defined

Because this is a book about *communication*, it makes sense to begin by defining that term. This isn't as simple as it might seem because people use the term in a variety of ways that are only vaguely related:

- A dog scratches at the back door, signaling its desire to be let out of the house.
- Data flow from one computer database to another in a cascade of electronic impulses.
- Strangers who live thousands of miles apart spot each other's postings on a social networking website, and they become friends through conversations via e-mail, text messaging, and instant messaging.
- Locals approach a group of confused-looking people who seem to be from out of town and ask if they can help.
- In her sermon, a religious leader encourages the congregation to get more involved in the community.

There is clearly some relationship among uses of the term such as these, but we need to narrow our focus before going on. A look at the table of contents of this book shows that it obviously doesn't deal with animals. Neither is it about Holy Communion, the bestowing of a material thing, or many of the other subjects mentioned in the *Oxford English Dictionary*'s 1,200-word definition of *communication*.

What, then, *are* we talking about when we use the term *communication*? As the reading on page 3 shows, there is no single, universally accepted usage. This isn't the place to explore the differences between these conceptions or to defend one against the others. What we need is a working definition that will help us in our study.

As its title suggests, this is a book about understanding *human* communication—so we'll start by explaining what it means to study communication that is unique to members of our species. For our purposes we'll define human **communication** as *the process of creating meaning through symbolic interaction*. Examining this definition reveals some important characteristics of human communication.

Communication Is a Process

We often talk about communication as if it occurred in discrete, individual acts such as one person's utterance or a conversation. In fact, communication is a continuous, ongoing process. Consider, for example, a friend's compliment about your appearance. Your interpretation of those words will depend on a long series of experiences stretching far back in time: How have others judged your appearance? How do you feel about your looks? How honest has your friend been in the past? How have you been feeling about one another recently? All this history will help shape your response to the friend's remark. In turn, the words you speak and the way you say them will shape the way your friend behaves toward you and others—both in this situation and in the future.

This simple example shows that it's inaccurate to talk about "acts" of communication as if they occurred in isolation. To put it differently, communication isn't a series of incidents pasted together like photographs in a scrapbook; instead, it is more like a motion picture in which the meaning comes from the unfolding of an interrelated series of images. The fact that communication is a process is reflected in the transactional model introduced later in this chapter.

INVITATION TO INSIGHT
The Many Meanings of Communication

Few words have as many meanings as communication. The term can refer to everything from messages on T-shirts to presidential speeches, from computer code to chimpanzee behavior. Communication has been the professional concern of philosophers, scientists (social, biological, and physical), poets, politicians, and entertainers, to name a few. Responding to this diversity, Brent Rubin asked, "How does being interested in communication differ from being interested in life?"

There are several reasons why the term *communication* has so many different meanings. Understanding them will help explain how and why this word refers to a broad range of subjects.

Interdisciplinary Heritage   Unlike most subjects, communication has captured the interest of scholars from a wide range of fields. Ever since classical times, philosophers have studied the meaning and significance of messages. In the twentieth century, social scientists have joined the field: Psychologists examine the causes and effects of communication as it relates to individuals. Sociologists and anthropologists examine how communication operates within and between societies and cultures. Political scientists explore the ways communication influences governmental affairs. Engineers use their skill to devise methods of conveying messages electronically. Zoologists focus on communication between animals. With this kind of diversity, it's no surprise that *communication* is a broad and sometimes confusing term.

Field and Activity   Sometimes the word *communication* refers to a field of study (of nonverbal messages or effects of televised violence on children, for example). In other cases it denotes an activity that people do. This confusion doesn't exist in most disciplines. People may study history or sociology, but they don't "historicate" or "sociologize." Having only one word that refers to both the field of study and the activity that it examines leads to confusion.

Humanity and Social Science   Unlike most disciplines, communication straddles two very different academic domains. It has one foot firmly planted in the humanities, where it shares concerns with disciplines like English and philosophy. At the same time, other scholars in the field take an approach like their colleagues in the social sciences, such as psychology, sociology, and anthropology. And to confuse matters even further, communication is sometimes associated with the performing arts, especially in the area of oral interpretation of literature.

Natural and Professional Communication   This is a natural activity that we all engage in unconsciously. At the same time, there are professional communication experts whose specialized duties require training and skill. Careers such as marketing, public relations, broadcasting, speechmaking, counseling, journalism, and management all call for talent that goes far beyond what is required for everyday speaking and listening.

Communication and Communications   Even the name of the field is confusing. Traditionally, *communications* (with an "s") has been used when referring to activities involving technology and the mass media. *Communication* is typically used to describe face-to-face and written messages, as well as the field as a whole. With the growth of communication technology, the two terms are being used interchangeably more often.

Brent Rubin
Communication and Human Behavior

Communication Is Symbolic

Symbols are used to represent things, processes, ideas, or events in ways that make communication possible. Chapter 3 discusses the nature of symbols in more detail, but this idea is so important that it needs an introduction now. The most significant feature of symbols is their *arbitrary* nature. For example, there's no logical reason why the letters in the word *book* should stand for the object you're reading now. Speakers of Spanish call it a *libro*, and Germans call it a *Buch*. Even in English, another term would work just as well as long as everyone agreed to use it in the same way. We overcome the arbitrary nature of symbols by linguistic rules and customs. Effective communication depends on agreement among people about these rules. This is easiest to see when we observe people who don't follow linguistic conventions. For example, recall how unusual the speech of children and nonnative speakers of a language often sounds.

Animals don't use symbols in the varied and complex ways that humans do. There's nothing symbolic about a dog scratching at the door to be let out; there is a natural connection between the door and the dog's goal. By contrast, the words in the human utterance "Open the door!" are only arbitrarily related to the request they represent.

Symbolic communication allows people to think or talk about the past (while cats have no concept of their ancestors from a century ago), explain the present (a trout can't warn its companions about its close call with a fishing hook), and speculate about the future (a crow has no awareness of the year 2025, let alone tomorrow).

Like words, some nonverbal behavior can have symbolic meaning. For example, to most North Americans, nodding your head up and down means "yes" (although this meaning isn't universal). But even more than words, many nonverbal behaviors are ambiguous. Does a frown signify anger or unhappiness? Does a hug stand for a friendly greeting or a symbol of the hugger's romantic interest in you? One can't always be sure. We'll discuss the ambiguous nature of nonverbal communication in Chapter 5.

CRITICAL THINKING PROBE

● **Must Communication Be Intentional?**

Some theorists believe that any behavior that has meaning to others should be considered communication, whether it is intentional or not. To them, an involuntary grimace or overheard remark is worthy of studying. Other scholars believe that only messages that are intentionally sent and received should be considered communication. They argue that the broader definition means that the study of communication has no boundaries. Which position do you take? Be prepared to support your viewpoint in a discussion with others who hold the opposing viewpoint.

Types of Communication

Within the domain of human interaction, there are several types of communication. Each occurs in a different context. Despite the features they all share, each has its own characteristics.

Intrapersonal Communication

By definition, **intrapersonal communication** means "communicating with oneself."[1] You can tune in to one way that each of us communicates internally by listening to the little voice that lives in your mind. Take a moment and listen to what it is saying. Try it now, before reading on. Did you hear it? It may have been saying something like "What little voice? I don't have any little voice!" This voice is the "sound" of your thinking.

We don't always think in verbal terms, but whether the process is apparent or not, the way we mentally process information influences our interaction with others. Even though intrapersonal communication doesn't include other people directly, it does affect almost every type of interaction. You can understand the role of intrapersonal communication by imagining your thoughts in each of the following situations.

- You are planning to approach a stranger whom you would like to get to know better.
- You pause a minute and look at the audience before beginning a ten-minute speech.
- The boss yawns while you are asking for a raise.
- A friend seems irritated lately, and you're not sure whether you are responsible.

CULTURAL IDIOM
tune in:
focus on

The way you handle all of these situations would depend on the intrapersonal communication that precedes or accompanies your overt behavior. Much of Chapter 2 deals with the perception process in everyday situations, and part of Chapter 12 focuses on the intrapersonal communication that can minimize anxiety when you deliver a speech.

Dyadic/Interpersonal Communication

Social scientists call two persons interacting a **dyad,** and they often use the term **dyadic communication** to describe this type of communication. Dyads are the most common communication setting. One study revealed that college students spend almost half of their total communication time interacting with one other person.[2] Observation in a variety of settings ranging from playgrounds, train depots, and shopping malls to other settings shows that most communication is dyadic in nature.[3] Even communication within larger groups (think of classrooms, parties, and families as examples) consists of multiple, often shifting dyadic encounters.

Dyadic interaction is sometimes considered identical to **interpersonal communication,** but as Chapter 6 explains, not all two-person interaction can be considered interpersonal in the fullest sense of the word. In fact, you will learn that the qualities that characterize interpersonal communication aren't limited to twosomes. They can be present in threesomes or even in small groups.

Small Group Communication

In **small group communication** every person can participate actively with the other members. Small groups are a common fixture of everyday life. Your family is a group. So are an athletic team, a group of coworkers in several time zones connected in cyberspace, and several students working on a class project.

Whatever their makeup, small groups possess characteristics that are not present in a dyad. For instance, in a group, the majority of members can put pressure on those in the minority to conform, either consciously or unconsciously, but in a dyad no such pressures exist. Conformity pressures can also be comforting, leading group members to take risks that they would not dare if they were alone or in a dyad. With their greater size, groups also have the ability to be more creative than dyads. Finally, communication in groups is affected strongly by the type of leader who is in a position of authority. Groups are such an important communication setting that Chapters 8 and 9 focus exclusively on them.

Public Communication

Public communication occurs when a group becomes too large for all members to contribute. One characteristic of public communication is an unequal amount of speaking. One or more people are likely to deliver their remarks to the remaining members, who act as an audience. This leads to a second characteristic of public settings: limited verbal feedback. The audience isn't able to talk back in a two-way conversation the way they might in a dyadic or small group setting. This doesn't mean that speakers operate in a vacuum when delivering their remarks. Audiences often have a chance to ask questions and offer brief comments, and their nonverbal reactions offer a wide range of clues about their reception of the speaker's remarks.

CULTURAL IDIOM

operate in a vacuum:
function as if there were no others around

Public speakers usually have a greater chance to plan and structure their remarks than do communicators in smaller settings. For this reason, several chapters of this book describe the steps you can take to prepare and deliver an effective speech.

Mass Communication

Mass communication consists of messages that are transmitted to large, widespread audiences via electronic and print media: newspapers, magazines, television, radio, blogs, websites, and so on. As you can see in the Mass Communication section of the *Understanding Human Communication* website, mass communication differs from the interpersonal, small group, and public varieties in several ways. First, most mass messages are aimed at a large audience without any personal contact between sender and receivers. Second, many of the messages sent via mass communication channels are developed, or at least financed, by large organizations. In this sense, mass communication is far less personal and more of a product than the other types we have examined so far. Finally, mass communication is often controlled by many gatekeepers who determine what messages will be delivered to consumers, how they will be constructed, and when they will be delivered. Sponsors (whether corporate or governmental), editors, producers, reporters, and executives all have the power to influence mass messages in ways that don't affect most other types. While blogs have given ordinary people the chance to reach enormous audiences, the bulk of mass messages are still controlled by corporate and governmental sources. Because of these and other unique characteristics, the study of mass communication raises special issues and deserves special treatment.

Functions of Communication

Now that we have a working understanding of the term *communication*, it is important to discuss why we will spend so much time exploring this subject. Perhaps the strongest argument for studying communication is its central role in our lives. The amount of time we spend communicating is staggering. In one study, researchers measured the amount of time a sample group of college students spent on various activities.[4] They found that the subjects spent an average of over 61 percent of their waking hours engaged in some form of communication. Whatever one's occupation, the results of such a study would not be too different. Most of us are surrounded by others, trying to understand them and hoping that they understand us: family, friends, coworkers, teachers, and strangers.

There's a good reason why we speak, listen, read, and write so much: Communication satisfies many of our needs.

Physical Needs

Communication is so important that it is necessary for physical health. In fact, evidence suggests that an absence of satisfying communication can even jeopardize life itself. Medical researchers have identified a wide range of hazards that result from a lack of close relationships.[5] For instance:

- People who lack strong relationships have two to three times the risk of early death, regardless of whether they smoke, drink alcoholic beverages, or exercise regularly.

- Terminal cancer strikes socially isolated people more often than those who have close personal relationships.

- Divorced, separated, and widowed people are five to ten times more likely to need hospitalization for mental problems than their married counterparts.

- Pregnant women under stress and without supportive relationships have three times more complications than pregnant women who suffer from the same stress but have strong social support.

- Socially isolated people are four times more susceptible to the common cold than those who have active social networks.[6]

Studies indicate that social isolation is a major risk factor contributing to coronary disease, comparable to physiological factors such as diet, cigarette smoking, obesity, and lack of physical activity.[7]

Research like this demonstrates the importance of having satisfying personal relationships. Remember: Not everyone needs the same amount of contact, and the quality of communication is almost certainly as important as the quantity. The important point here is that personal communication is essential for our well-being. To paraphrase an old song, "people who need people" aren't "the luckiest people in the world," they're the *only* people!

Identity Needs

Communication does more than enable us to survive. It is the way—indeed, the *only* way—we learn who we are. As you'll read in Chapter 2, our sense of identity comes from the way we interact with other people. Are we smart or stupid, attractive or ugly, skillful or inept? The answers to these questions don't come from looking in the mirror. We decide who we are based on how others react to us.

Deprived of communication with others, we would have no sense of identity. This fact is illustrated by the case of the famous "Wild Boy of Aveyron," who spent his early childhood without any apparent human contact. The boy was discovered in January 1800 while digging for vegetables in a French village garden.[8] He showed no behaviors one would expect in a social human. The boy could not speak but uttered only weird cries. More significant than this absence of social skills was his lack of any identity as a human being. As author Roger Shattuck put it, "The boy had no human sense of being in the world. He had no sense of himself as a person related to other persons."[9] Only after the influence of a loving "mother" did the boy begin to behave—and, we can imagine, think of himself as a human. Contemporary stories support the essential role that communication plays in shaping identity. In 1970, authorities discovered a twelve-year-old girl (whom they called "Genie") who had spent virtually all her life in an otherwise empty, darkened bedroom with almost no human contact. The child could not speak and had no sense of herself as a person until she was removed from her family and "nourished" by a team of caregivers.[10]

Like Genie and the boy of Aveyron, each of us enters the world with little or no sense of identity. We gain an idea of who we are from the ways others define us. As Chapter 2 explains, the messages we receive in early childhood are the strongest, but the influence of others continues throughout life. Chapter 2 also explains how we use communication to manage the way others view us.

Social Needs

Besides helping to define who we are, communication provides a vital link with others. Researchers and theorists have identified a range of social needs we satisfy by communicating: *pleasure* (e.g., "because it's fun," "to have a good time"); *affection* (e.g., "to help others," "to let others know I care"); *inclusion* (e.g., "because I need someone to talk to or be with," "because it makes me less lonely"); *escape* (e.g., "to put off doing something I should be doing"); *relaxation* (e.g., "because it allows me to unwind"); and *control* (e.g., "because I want someone to do something for me," "to get something I don't have").[11]

As you look at this list of social needs for communicating, imagine how empty your life would be if these needs weren't satisfied. Then notice that it would be impossible to fulfill them without communicating with others. Because relationships with others are so vital, some theorists have gone as far as to argue that communication is the primary goal of human existence. Anthropologist Walter Goldschmidt terms the drive for meeting social needs as the "human career."[12]

Practical Needs

We shouldn't overlook the everyday, important functions that communication serves. Communication is the tool that lets us tell the hair stylist to take just a little off the sides, direct the doctor to where it hurts, and inform the plumber that the broken pipe needs attention *now*!

Beyond these obvious needs, a wealth of research demonstrates that communication is an important key to effectiveness in a variety of everyday settings. For example, a survey of over four hundred employers identified "communication skills" as the top characteristic that employers seek in job candidates.[13] It was rated as more important than technical competence, work experience, or academic background. In another survey, over 90 percent of the personnel officials at five hundred U.S. businesses stated that increased communication skills are needed for success in the twenty-first century.[14]

Communication is just as important outside of work. College roommates who are both willing and able to communicate effectively report higher satisfaction with one another than do those who lack these characteristics.[15] Married couples who were identified as effective communicators reported happier relationships than did less skillful husbands and wives.[16] In school, the grade point averages of college students were related positively to their communication competence.[17] In "getting acquainted" situations, communication competence played a major role in whether a person was judged physically attractive, socially desirable, and good at the task of getting acquainted.[18]

Modeling Communication

So far we have introduced a basic definition of *communication* and seen the functions it performs. This information is useful, but it only begins to describe the process we will be examining throughout this book. One way to understand more about what it means to communicate is to look at some models that describe what happens when two or more people interact. As you will see, over the last half-century scholars have developed an increasingly accurate and sophisticated view of this process.

A Linear Model

Until about fifty years ago, researchers viewed communication as something that one person "does" to another.[19] In this **linear communication model,** communication is like giving an injection: a **sender encodes** ideas and feelings into some sort of **message** and then conveys them to a **receiver** who **decodes** them. (Figure 1-1.)

One important element of the linear model is the communication **channel**—the method by which a message is conveyed between people. For most people, face-to-face contact is the most familiar and obvious channel. Writing is another channel. In addition to these long-used forms, **mediated communication** channels include telephone, e-mail, instant messaging, faxes, voice mail, and even videoconferencing. (The word *mediated* reflects the fact that these messages are conveyed through some sort of communication medium.)

The channel you choose can make a big difference in the effect of a message. For example, a typewritten love letter probably wouldn't have the same effect as a hand-written note or card. Likewise, ending a relationship by sending a text message to your lover's cell phone would make a very different statement than delivering the bad news in person.

The linear model also introduces the concept of **noise**—a term used by social scientists to describe any forces that interfere with effective communication. Noise can occur at every stage of the communication process. Three types of noise can disrupt communication—external, physiological, and psychological. *External noise* (also called "*physical*") includes those factors outside the receiver that make it difficult to hear, as well as many other kinds of distractions. For instance, too much cigarette smoke in a crowded room might make it hard for you to pay attention to another person, and sitting in the rear of an auditorium might make a speaker's remarks unclear. External noise can disrupt communication almost anywhere in our model—in the sender, channel, message, or receiver. *Physiological noise* involves biological factors in the receiver or sender that interfere with accurate reception: illness, fatigue, and so

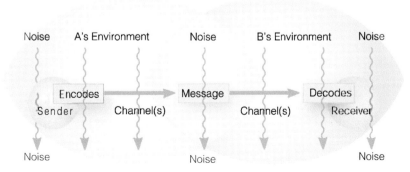

FIGURE 1-1   Linear Communication Model

on. *Psychological noise* refers to forces within a communicator that interfere with the ability to express or understand a message accurately. For instance, an outdoors person might exaggerate the size and number of the fish he caught in order to convince himself and others of his talents. In the same way, a student might become so upset upon learning that she failed a test that she would be unable (perhaps *unwilling* is a better word) to understand clearly where she went wrong.

A linear model shows that communicators often occupy different **environments**—fields of experience that help them understand others' behavior. In communication terminology, *environment* refers not only to a physical location but also to the personal experiences and cultural backgrounds that participants bring to a conversation.

Consider just some of the factors that might contribute to different environments:

- A might belong to one ethnic group and B to another;
- A might be rich and B poor;
- A might be in a rush and B have nowhere to go;
- A might have lived a long, eventful life, and B might be young and inexperienced;
- A might be passionately concerned with the subject and B indifferent to it.

Notice how the model in Figure 1-1 shows that the environments of A and B overlap. This area represents the background that the communicators must have in common. As the shared environment becomes smaller, communication becomes more difficult. Consider a few examples in which different perspectives can make understanding difficult:

- Bosses who have trouble understanding the perspective of their employees will be less effective managers, and workers who do not appreciate the challenges of being a boss are more likely to be uncooperative (and probably less suitable for advancement).
- Parents who have trouble recalling their youth are likely to clash with their children, who have never known and may not appreciate the responsibility that comes with parenting.
- Members of a dominant culture who have never experienced how it feels to be "different" may not appreciate the concerns of people from nondominant cocultures, whose own perspectives make it hard to understand the cultural blindness of the majority.

Differing environments make understanding others challenging but certainly not impossible. Hard work and many of the skills described in this book provide ways to bridge the gap that separates all of us to a greater or lesser degree. For now, recognizing the challenge that comes from dissimilar environments is a good start. You can't solve a problem until you recognize that it exists.

A Transactional Model

Despite its simplicity, the linear model doesn't do a very good job of representing the way most communication operates. The **transactional communication model** in Figure 1-2 presents a more accurate picture in several respects.

Simultaneous Sending and Receiving   Although some types of mass communication do flow in a one-way, linear manner, most types of personal communication are two-way exchanges.[20] The transactional model reflects the fact that we usually send and

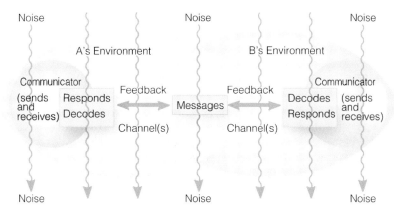

FIGURE 1-2   Transactional Communication Model

receive messages simultaneously. The roles of sender and receiver that seemed separate in the linear model are now superimposed and redefined as those of "communicators." This new term reflects the fact that at a given moment we are capable of receiving, decoding, and responding to another person's behavior, while at the same time that other person is receiving and responding to ours.

Consider, for instance, the significance of a friend's yawn as you describe your romantic problems. Or imagine the blush you may see as you tell one of your raunchier jokes to a new acquaintance. Nonverbal behaviors like these show that most face-to-face communication is a two-way affair. The discernible response of a receiver to a sender's message is called **feedback.** Not all feedback is nonverbal, of course. Sometimes it is oral, as when you ask an instructor questions about an upcoming test or volunteer your opinion of a friend's new haircut. In other cases it is written, as when you answer the questions on a midterm exam or respond to a letter from a friend. Figure 1-2 makes the importance of feedback clear. It shows that most communication is, indeed, a two-way affair.

Some forms of mediated communication like e-mail and text messaging don't appear to be simultaneous. Even here, though, the process is more complicated than the linear model suggests. For example, if you've ever waited impatiently for the response to a text message or instant message, you understand that even a nonresponse can have symbolic meaning. Is the unresponsive recipient busy? Thoughtful? Offended? Indifferent? Whether or not your interpretation is accurate, the silence is a form of communication.

Another weakness of the traditional linear model is the questionable assumption that all communication involves encoding. We certainly do choose symbols to convey most verbal messages. But what about the many nonverbal cues that occur whether or not people speak: facial expressions, gestures, postures, vocal tones, and so on? Cues like these clearly do offer information about others, although they are often unconscious and thus don't involve encoding. For this reason, the transactional model replaces the term *encodes* with the broader term *responds*, because it describes both intentional and unintentional actions that can be observed and interpreted.[21]

Communication Is Fluid, Not Static   It's difficult to isolate a discrete "act" of communication from the events that precede and follow it. The way a friend or family member reacts to a sarcastic remark you make will probably depend on the way you have related to one another in the past. Likewise, the way you'll act toward each other in the future depends on the outcome of this conversation.

CULTURAL IDIOM

pin the blame:
claim the fault lies with

Communication Is Relational, Not Individual The transactional model shows that communication isn't something we do *to* others; rather, it is something we do *with* them. In this sense, communication is rather like dancing—at least the kind of dancing we do with partners. Like dancing, communication depends on the involvement of a partner. And like good dancing, successful communication isn't something that depends just on the skill of one person. A great dancer who doesn't consider and adapt to the skill level of his or her partner can make both people look bad. In communication and dancing, even two talented partners don't guarantee success. When two talented dancers perform without coordinating their movements, the results feel bad to the dancers and look foolish to an audience. Finally, relational communication—like dancing—is a unique creation that arises out of the way in which the partners interact. The way you dance probably varies from one partner to another because of its cooperative, transactional nature. Likewise, the way you communicate almost certainly varies with different partners.

Psychologist Kenneth Gergen captures the relational nature of communication well when he points out how our success depends on interaction with others. As he says, ". . . one cannot be 'attractive' without others who are attracted, a 'leader' without others willing to follow, or a 'loving person' without others to affirm with appreciation."[22]

Because communication is transactional, it's often a mistake to suggest that just one person is responsible for a relationship. Consider the accompanying cartoon. Both Cathy and Irving had good intentions, and both probably could have handled the situation better. As the humorous outcome shows, trying to pin the blame for a disappointing outcome on one person or the other is fruitless and counterproductive. It would have been far better to ask, "How did *we* handle this situation poorly, and what can *we* do to make it better?"

The transactional nature of communication shows up in school, where teachers and students influence one another's behavior. For example, teachers who regard some students negatively may treat them with subtle or overt disfavor. As a result, these students are likely to react to their teachers' behavior negatively, which reinforces the teachers' original attitudes and expectations.[23] It isn't necessary to resolve the "who started it" issue here to recognize that the behaviors of teachers and students are part of a transactional relationship.

The transactional character of communication also figures dramatically in relationships between parents and their children. We normally think of "good parenting" in terms of how well children turn out. But research suggests that the quality of interaction between parents and children is a two-way affair, that children influence parents just as much as the other way around.[24] For example, children who engage in what social scientists call "problematic behavior" evoke more high-control responses from their parents than do cooperative

children. By contrast, youngsters with mild temperaments are less likely to provoke coercive reactions by their parents than are more aggressive children. Parents with low self-esteem tend to send more messages that weaken the self-esteem of their children, who in turn are likely to act in ways that make the parents feel even worse about themselves. Thus, a mutually reinforcing cycle arises in which parents and children shape one another's feelings and behavior. In cases like this it's at least difficult and probably impossible to identify who is the "sender" and who is the "receiver" of messages. It's more accurate to acknowledge that parents and children—just like husbands and wives, bosses and employees, teachers and students, or any other people who communicate with one another—act in ways that mutually influence one another.

By now you can see that a transactional model of communication should be more like a motion picture film than a gallery of still photographs. Although Figure 1-2 does a fair job of picturing the phenomenon we call communication, an animated version in which the environments, communicators, and messages constantly change would be an even better way of capturing the process.

Communication Competence: What Makes an Effective Communicator?

It's easy to recognize good communicators, and even easier to spot poor ones. But what are the characteristics that distinguish effective communicators from their less successful counterparts? Answering this question has been one of the leading challenges for communication scholars.[25] Although all the answers aren't yet in, research has identified a great deal of important and useful information about communication competence.

Communication Competence Defined

Although scholars are still working to clarify the nature of **communication competence,** most would agree that effective communication involves achieving one's goals in a manner that, ideally, maintains or enhances the relationship in which it occurs.[26] This definition suggests several important characteristics of communication competence.

There Is No "Ideal" Way to Communicate   Your own experience shows that a variety of communication styles can be effective. Some very successful people are serious, whereas others use humor; some are gregarious, whereas others are quiet; and some are straightforward, whereas others hint diplomatically. Just as there are many kinds of beautiful music and art, there are many kinds of competent communication.

The type of communication that succeeds in one situation might be a colossal blunder in another. The joking insults you routinely trade with a friend might be insensitive and discouraging if he or she had just suffered a personal setback. The language you use with your peers might offend a family member, and last Saturday night's romantic approach would probably be out of place at work on Monday morning. For this reason, being a competent communicator requires flexibility in understanding what approach is likely to work best in a given situation.[27]

"I SAID, 'I have trouble developing close relationships with people!' For cryin' out loud, clean out your ears, fathead!"

MEDIA ROOM
Communication Competence and Incompetence

Characters in films and television are often walking examples of communication competence . . . and incompetence. By watching these portrayals, you can gain insights about your own communication skills.

In the TV series *The Office,* Michael Scott (Steve Carell) is a boss who believes he is funny, lovable, and a fountain of business wisdom. In actuality, Michael's misguided sense of humor and bumbling management style make him an object of ridicule among his staff. His miscues are often hilarious, but Michael shows how poor self-monitoring can lead to incompetent communication.

In *Sideways,* two clueless friends suffer the consequences of their communicative incompetence during a road trip to the California wine country. Neurotic Miles (Paul Giamatti) describes his favorite wine grape, Pinot Noir, as "thin skinned and temperamental," but he might as well be referring to himself. Jack (Thomas Hayden Church) would rather make another sexual conquest than tell the truth—most importantly, that his marriage is less than a week away. It's easy to laugh at the blunders of this odd pair of friends, but it's clear that Miles's hypersensitivity and Jack's dishonesty doom them to a life of failed relationships.

Erin Brockovich is competent in some contexts, but not others. Her argumentative style and tenacious personality make her a successful public interest advocate who wins millions of settlement dollars for the people she represents, but the same traits prevent her from having successful personal relationships. Erin loses a boyfriend who loves and supports her, offends coworkers, rarely sees her children, and almost gets fired on several occasions. Like Erin, most of us need to recognize how to use our strengths and overcome our limitations if we want to become successful communicators.

New Zealander Burt Munro (Anthony Hopkins) in *World's Fastest Indian* meets a diverse array of characters while pursuing his dream to race at Utah's Bonneville Salt Flats. Those characters include a motorcycle gang, transvestite hotel clerk, Latino car salesman, Native American who lives in the desert, and a U.S. Air Force officer on leave from dropping napalm in Vietnam. In all these encounters, Burt shows how open-mindedness and tolerance for ambiguity can turn potential adversaries into friends.

The Office (2005–   , Rated TV-14)

Sideways (2004, Rated R)

Erin Brockovich (2000, Rated R)

World's Fastest Indian (2006, Rated PG-13)

For more resources about communication in film and television, see *Now Playing* at the *Understanding Human Communication* website at www.oup.com/us/uhc10.

Competence Is Situational   Because competent behavior varies so much from one situation and person to another, it's a mistake to think that communication competence is a trait that a person either possesses or lacks. It's more accurate to talk about *degrees* or *areas* of competence.[28] You and the people you know are probably quite competent in some areas and less so in others. You might deal quite skillfully with peers, for example, but feel clumsy interacting with people much older or younger, wealthier or poorer, or more or less attractive than yourself. In fact, your competence with one person may vary from one situation to another. This means that it's an overgeneralization to say, in a moment of distress, "I'm a terrible communicator!" It would be more accurate to say, "I didn't handle this situation very well, even though I'm better in others."

Competence Is Relational   Because communication is transactional, something we do with others rather than to them, behavior that is competent in one relationship isn't necessarily competent in others.

A fascinating study on relational satisfaction illustrates that what constitutes satisfying communication varies from one relationship to another.[29] Researchers Brent Burleson and Wendy Sampter hypothesized that people with sophisticated communication skills (such as managing conflict well, giving ego-support to others, and providing comfort to relational partners) would be better at maintaining friendships than would be less skilled communicators. To their surprise, the results did not support this hypothesis. In fact, friendships were most satisfying when partners possessed matching skill levels. Apparently, relational satisfaction arises in part when our style matches those of the people with whom we interact.

The same principle holds true in the case of jealousy. Researchers have uncovered a variety of ways by which people deal with jealousy in their relationships.[30] The ways included keeping closer tabs on the partner, acting indifferent, decreasing affection, talking the matter over, and acting angry. The researchers found that no type of behavior was effective or ineffective in every relationship. They concluded that approaches that work with some people would be harmful to others. Findings like these demonstrate that competence arises out of developing ways of interacting that work for you and for the other people involved.[31]

Competence Can Be Learned   To some degree, biology is destiny when it comes to communication style.[32] Studies of identical and fraternal twins suggest that traits including sociability, anger, and relaxation seem to be partially a function of our genetic makeup. Fortunately, biology isn't the only factor that shapes how we communicate: Communication is a set of skills that anyone can learn. As children grow, their ability to communicate effectively develops. For example, older children can produce more sophisticated persuasive attempts than can younger ones.[33] Along with maturity, systematic education (such as the class in which you are now enrolled) can boost communicative competence. Even a modest amount of training can produce dramatic results. After only thirty minutes of instruction, one group of observers became significantly more effective in detecting deception in interviews.[34] One study revealed that college students' communication competence increases over their undergraduate studies.[35] Even without systematic training, it's possible to develop communication skills through the processes of trial-and-error and observation. We learn from our own successes and failures, as well as from observing other models—both positive and negative.

Characteristics of Competent Communicators

Although competent communication varies from one situation to another, scholars have identified several common denominators that characterize effective communication in most contexts.

A Wide Range of Behaviors   Effective communicators are able to choose their actions from a wide range of behaviors. To understand the importance of having a large communication repertoire, imagine that someone you know repeatedly tells jokes—perhaps discriminatory ones—that you find offensive. You could respond to these jokes in a number of ways. You could:

- Say nothing, figuring that the risks of bringing the subject up would be greater than the benefits.
- Ask a third party to say something to the joke teller about the offensiveness of the jokes.
- Hint at your discomfort, hoping that your friend would get the point.
- Joke about your friend's insensitivity, counting on humor to soften the blow of your criticism.
- Express your discomfort in a straightforward way, asking your friend to stop telling the offensive jokes, at least around you.
- Simply demand that your friend stop.

With this choice of responses at your disposal (and you can probably think of others as well), you could pick the one that had the best chance of success. But if you were able to use only one or two of these responses when raising a delicate issue—always keeping quiet or always hinting, for example—your chances of success would be much smaller. Indeed, many poor communicators are easy to spot by their limited range of responses. Some are chronic jokers. Others are always belligerent. Still others are quiet in almost every situation. Like a piano player who knows only one tune or a chef who can prepare only a few dishes, these people are forced to rely on a small range of responses again and again, whether or not they are successful.

Ability to Choose the Most Appropriate Behavior   Simply possessing a large array of communication skills isn't a guarantee of effectiveness. It's also necessary to know which of these skills will work best in a particular situation. Choosing the best way to send a message is rather like choosing a gift: What is appropriate for one person won't be appropriate for another one at all. This ability to choose the best approach is essential because a response that works well in one setting would flop miserably in another one.

Although it's impossible to say precisely how to act in every situation, there are at least three factors to consider when you are deciding which response to choose: the context, your goal, and the other person.

Skill at Performing Behaviors   After you have chosen the most appropriate way to communicate, it's still necessary to perform the required skills effectively. There is a big difference between knowing *about* a skill and being able to put it into practice. Simply being aware of alternatives isn't much help, unless you can skillfully put these alternatives to work.

Just reading about communication skills in the following chapters won't guarantee that you can start using them flawlessly. As with any other skills—playing a musical instrument or learning a sport, for example—the road to competence in communication is not a short one. You can expect that your first efforts at communicating differently will be awkward. After some practice you will become more skillful, although you will still have to think about the new way of speaking or listening. Finally, after repeating the new skill again and again, you will find you can perform it without conscious thought.

Empathy/Perspective Taking   People have the best chance of developing an effective message when they understand the other person's point of view. And because others aren't always good at expressing their thoughts and feelings clearly, the ability to imagine how an issue might look from the other's point of view is an important skill. The value of taking the other's perspective suggests one reason why listening is so important. Not only does it help us understand others, but also it gives us information to develop strategies about how to best influence them. Because empathy is such an important element of communicative competence, much of Chapter 4 is devoted to this topic.

Cognitive Complexity   Cognitive complexity is the ability to construct a variety of frameworks for viewing an issue. Cognitive complexity is an ingredient of communication competence because it allows us to make sense of people using a variety of perspectives. For instance, imagine that a longtime friend seems to be angry with you. One possible explanation is that your friend is offended by something you've done. Another possibility is that something upsetting has happened in another part of your

Calvin and Hobbes   by Bill Watterson

Source: CALVIN and HOBBES © 1994 Watterson. Distributed by UNIVERSAL PRESS SYNDICATE. Reprinted with permission. All Rights Reserved.

friend's life. Or perhaps nothing at all is wrong, and you're just being overly sensitive. Researchers have found that the ability to analyze the behavior of others in a variety of ways leads to greater "conversational sensitivity," increasing the chances of acting in ways that will produce satisfying results.[36]

Self-Monitoring Psychologists use the term *self-monitoring* to describe the process of paying close attention to one's behavior and using these observations to shape the way one behaves. Self-monitors are able to separate a part of their consciousness and observe their behavior from a detached viewpoint, making observations such as:

"I'm making a fool out of myself."

"I'd better speak up now."

"This approach is working well. I'll keep it up."

Chapter 2 explains how too much self-monitoring can be problematic. Still, people who are aware of their behavior and the impression it makes are more skillful communicators than people who are low self-monitors.[37] For example, they are more accurate in judging others' emotional states, better at remembering information about others, less shy, and more assertive. By contrast, low self-monitors aren't even able to recognize their incompetence. (Calvin, in the nearby cartoon, does a nice job of illustrating this problem.) One study revealed that poor communicators were blissfully ignorant of their shortcomings and more likely to overestimate their skill than were better communicators.[38] For example, experimental subjects who scored in the lowest quartile on joke-telling skill were more likely than their funnier counterparts to grossly overestimate their sense of humor.

Commitment to the Relationship One feature that distinguishes effective communication in almost any context is commitment. People who seem to care about the relationship communicate better than those who don't.[39] This concern shows up in commitment to the other person and to the message you are expressing.

Intercultural Communication Competence

What qualifies as competent behavior in one culture might be completely inept or even offensive in another.[40] On an obvious level, customs like belching after a meal or appearing nude in public, which might be appropriate in some parts of the world, would be considered outrageous in others. But as the "Understanding Diversity" box on page 19 shows, there are more subtle differences in competent communication. For example, qualities like being self-disclosing and speaking directly that are valued in the United States are likely to be considered overly aggressive and insensitive in many Asian cultures, where subtlety and indirectness are considered important.[41]

Cultures and Co-Cultures   National differences aren't the only dimensions of culture. Within a society, co-cultures have different communication practices. Consider just a few examples of co-cultures:

  age (e.g., teen, Gen X, baby boomer)

  socioeconomic status (e.g., high or low income; little or much education)

  race/ethnicity (e.g., Native American, Latino)

  sexual orientation (e.g., lesbian, gay male)

  national heritage (e.g., Puerto Rican, Vietnamese)

  different physical abilities (e.g., wheelchair users, deaf)

  religion (e.g., Latter Day Saints, Muslim)

  lifestyle (e.g., biker, gamer)

Some scholars have even characterized men and women as belonging to different co-cultures, claiming that each gender's style of communication is distinct. We'll have more to say about that topic throughout this book.

Members of various co-cultures may have different notions of appropriate behavior. One study revealed that ideas of how good friends should communicate varied from one ethnic group to another.[42] As a group, Latinos valued relational support most highly, whereas African Americans valued respect and acceptance. Asian Americans emphasized a caring, positive exchange of ideas, and Anglo Americans prized friends who recognized their needs as individuals. Findings like these mean that there can be no surefire list of rules or tips that will guarantee your success as a communicator. They also suggest that competent communicators are able to adapt their style to suit the individual and cultural preferences of others.[43]

Characteristics of Intercultural Competence   Communicating successfully with people from different cultural backgrounds calls for the same elements of competence outlined in the pages you have just read. But beyond these basic qualities, communication researchers have identified several other especially important ingredients of successful intercultural communication.[44]

Most obviously, it helps to know the rules of a specific culture. For example, the kind of self-deprecating humor that Americans are likely to find amusing may fall flat among Arabs from the Middle East.[45] But beyond knowing the specific rules of an individual culture, there are also attitudes and skills called "culture general" that help communicators build relationships with people from other backgrounds.[46]

Motivation   The desire to communicate successfully with strangers is an important start. For example, people high in willingness to communicate with people from other cultures report a greater number of friends from different backgrounds than those who are less willing to reach out.[47] Having the proper motivation is important in all communication, but particularly so in intercultural interactions because they can be quite challenging.

UNDERSTANDING DIVERSITY

Call Centers and Culture

In a sleek new office building, two dozen young Indians are studying the customs of a place none of them has ever seen. One by one, the students present their conclusions about this fabled land.

"Americans eat a lot of junk food. Table manners are very casual,"says Ritu Khanna.

"People are quite self-centered. The average American has 13 credit cards," says Nerissa Dcosta.

"Seventy-six percent of the people mistrust the government. In the near future, this figure is expected to go up to 100 percent," says Sunny Trama.

The Indians, who range in age from 20 to 27, have been hired to take calls from cranky or distraught Americans whose computers have gone haywire. To do this, they need to communicate in a language that is familiar but a culture that is foreign.

"We're not saying India is better or America is better," says their trainer, Alefiya Rangwala. "We just want to be culturally sensitive so there's no disconnect when someone phones for tech support."

Call centers took root here during the 2001 recession, when U.S. companies were struggling to control expenses. By firing American customer service workers and hiring Indians, the firms slashed their labor costs by 75%.

At first, training was simple. The centers gave employees names that were acceptable to American ears, with Arjun becoming Aaron and Sangita becoming Susan. The new hires were instructed to watch "Friends"and "Ally McBeal" to get an idea of American folkways.

But whether Aaron and Susan were repairing computers, selling long-distance service or fulfilling orders for diet tapes, problems immediately cropped up. The American callers often wanted a better deal or an impossibly swift resolution and were aggressive and sometimes abrasive about saying so.

The Indians responded according to their own deepest natures: They were silent when they didn't understand, and they often committed to more than their employers could deliver. They would tell the Americans that someone would get back to them tomorrow to check on their problems, and no one would.

Customer satisfaction plummeted. The U.S. clients grew alarmed. Some even returned their business to U.S. call centers.

Realizing that a new multibillion-dollar industry with 150,000 employees was at risk, Indian call centers have recently embarked on much more comprehensive training. New hires are taught how to express empathy, strategies to successfully open and close conversations, and above all how to be assertive, however unnatural it might feel.

"We like to please," says Aparajita Ajit, whose title is "head of talent transformation" for the call-center firm Mphasis. "It's very difficult for us to say no."

Originally, the ever-agreeable Indian agents had a hard time getting people to pay bills that were six months overdue. Too often, says trainer Deepa Nagraj, the calls would go like this:

"Hi," the Indian would say. "I'd like to set up a payment to get your account current. Can I help you do that?"

"No," the American responds.

"OK, let me know if you change your mind," the Indian says and hangs up.

Now, says Nagraj, the agents take no excuses.

David Streitfeld

Tolerance for Ambiguity   Communicating with people from different backgrounds can be confusing. A tolerance for ambiguity makes it possible to accept, and even embrace, the often equivocal and sometimes downright incomprehensible messages that characterize intercultural communication.

For instance, if you happen to work with colleagues raised in traditional Native American co-cultures, you may find them much quieter and less outgoing than you are used to. Your first reaction might be to chalk this reticence up to a lack of friendliness. However, it may be a reflection of a co-culture in which reticence is valued more than extroversion and silence more than loquacity. In cross-cultural situations like this, ambiguity is a fact of life, and a challenge.

Open-Mindedness   It's one thing to tolerate ambiguity; it's another thing to become open-minded about cultural differences. There is a natural tendency to view others' communication choices as "wrong" when they don't match our cultural upbringing. In some parts of the world, you may find that women are not regarded with the same attitude of equality that is common in the West. Likewise, in other cultures, you may be aghast at the casual tolerance of poverty beyond anything at home, or with a practices of bribery that don't jibe with homegrown notions of what is ethical. In situations like these, principled communicators aren't likely to compromise deeply held beliefs about what is right. At the same time, competence requires an attitude that recognizes that people who behave differently are most likely following rules that have governed their whole lives. Chapter 2 will offer more guidance on the challenges of viewing the world from others' perspectives.

Knowledge and Skill   The rules and customs that work with one group might be quite different from those that succeed with another. For example, when traveling in Latin America, you are likely to find that meetings there usually don't begin or end at their scheduled time, and that it takes the participants quite a while to "get down to business." Rather than viewing your hosts as irresponsible and unproductive, you'll want to recognize that the meaning of time is not the same in all cultures. Likewise, the gestures others make, the distance they stand from you, and the eye contact they maintain have ambiguous meanings that you'll need to learn and follow.

One way to boost your understanding of cultural differences is via **mindfulness**—awareness of your own behavior and that of others.[48] Communicators who lack this quality blunder through intercultural encounters mindlessly, oblivious of how their own behavior may confuse or offend others, and how behavior that they consider weird may be simply different. Communication theorist Charles Berger outlines three strategies for moving toward a more mindful, competent style of intercultural communication.[49]

- *Passive observation* involves noticing what behaviors members of a different culture use and applying these insights to communicate in ways that are most effective.

- *Active strategies* include reading, watching films, and asking experts and members of the other culture how to behave, as well as taking academic courses related to intercultural communication and diversity.[50]

- *Self-disclosure* involves volunteering personal information to people from the other culture with whom you want to communicate. One type of self-disclosure is to confess your cultural ignorance: "This is very new to me. What's the right thing to do in this situation?" This approach is the riskiest of the three described here, since some cultures may not value candor and self-disclosure as much as others. Nevertheless, most people are pleased when strangers attempt to learn the practices of their culture, and they are usually more than willing to offer information and assistance.

Competence in Mediated Communication

Since the early 1990s, a growing number of researchers and theorists have studied the phenomenon of *mediated communication:* technologies that connect people who communicate without being face to face. Some forms of mediated communication are Internet-based: E-mail, instant messaging, and social networking websites are examples. These typically are labeled *computer-mediated communication* (CMC). Other mediated channels are phone-based: Cell phone conversations and text messaging are among the most common forms. As the "Understanding Communication Technology" box on page 21 shows, mediated communication calls for some skills that are different from those necessary in face-to-face interaction.[51]

UNDERSTANDING COMMUNICATION TECHNOLOGY

What 2 Say When U Know 2 Much?
Social Networking Sites Demand a Set of New (Unwritten) Etiquette Rules

Christine Reus is a self-professed stalker—a "Facebook stalker," that is. "I meet new people, and that's the worst, because I've seen them on Facebook. I know all about their life and who they're dating, but I have to pretend I know nothing about them," says Reus, 21, a Vanderbilt student from Birmingham, Ala.

She says she doesn't worry if casual acquaintances know everything about her; her online profile shows her cell phone number, e-mail address, screen name, campus post-office box and 153 pictures of her with friends and a boyfriend. She would list her dorm's suite number, too, she says, but that's against sorority rules designed to protect her personal safety.

In this age of ubiquitous social networking sites such as My-Space and Facebook, casual "stalking" of friends and acquaintances is typical, if not implicitly encouraged. But just because people know intimate details about acquaintances' lives does not necessarily make it OK to mention it when they see each other in person. Users are expected to abide by an unwritten code of conduct that applies both online and offline. Problem is, these rules of etiquette are, well, unwritten.

With so much personal information online, it can be hard to separate what you've assimilated through face-to-face interaction from what you've gleaned online. The secret lies in not slipping up when you see real people. Reus says the formula is simple: With close friends, it is always OK to comment on their profiles; they expect it and might even be upset if you don't. With distant acquaintances, it is almost never OK. It's those in the middle that are tricky; it's OK to bring up their profiles only if there is a reasonable explanation for why you were looking at it in the first place. Mutual friends are a good excuse; it is perfectly plausible that you were looking at your friend's pictures—which this other person just happened to be in and which link to his or her profile. In any case, it's always possible to extricate yourself from an awkward situation by joking about how creepy Facebook stalking really is.

Byron Dubow, *USA Today*, March 8, 2007, p. 4D. http://www.usatoday.com/printedition/life/20070308/bl_cover08.art.htm

Challenges of Mediated Communication Nobody would downplay the challenges of communicating in face-to-face situations. But communicating via the Internet or phone presents its own set of issues.

Leaner Messages Social scientists use the term **richness** to describe the abundance of nonverbal cues that add clarity to a verbal message. Face-to-face communication is rich because it abounds with nonverbal cues that give communicators cues about the meanings of one another's words and offer hints about their feelings.[52] By comparison, most mediated communication is a much leaner channel for conveying information.

To appreciate how message richness varies by medium, imagine you haven't heard from a friend in several weeks and you decide to ask "Is anything wrong?" Your friend replies, "No, I'm fine." Would that response be more or less descriptive depending on whether you received it via text message, over the phone, or in person?

You almost certainly would be able to tell a great deal more from a face-to-face response because it would contain a richer array of cues: facial expressions, vocal tone, and so on. By contrast, a text message contains only words. The phone message—containing vocal, but no visual cues—would probably fall somewhere in between.

Because most mediated messages are leaner than the face-to-face variety, they can be harder to interpret with confidence. Irony and attempts at humor can easily be misunderstood, so as a receiver it's important to clarify your interpretations before jumping to conclusions. As a sender, think about how to send unambiguous messages so you aren't misunderstood. (We'll discuss the value of "emoticons" and other text-based cues in Chapters 3 and 5.)

Disinhibition   Sooner or later most of us speak before we think, blurting out remarks that embarrass ourselves and offend others. The tendency to transmit uncensored messages can be especially great in online communication, where we don't see, hear, or sometimes even know the target of our remarks. This **disinhibition** can take two forms.

Sometimes online communicators volunteer personal information that they would prefer to keep confidential from at least some receivers. Consider the example of social networking sites like Facebook, MySpace, and Friendster. A quick scan of home pages there shows that many users post text and images about themselves that could prove embarrassing in some contexts: "Here I am just before my DUI arrest." "This is me in Cancun on spring break." This is not the sort of information most people would be eager to show a prospective employer or certain family members.

A second form of disinhibition is increased expressiveness. A growing body of research shows that communicators are more direct—often in a critical way—when using mediated channels than in face-to-face contact.[53]

Sometimes communicators take disinhibition to the extreme, blasting off angry—even vicious—e-mails, text messages, and website postings. The common term for these outbursts is *flaming*. Here is the account of one writer who was the target of an obscenity-filled e-mail:

> No one had ever said something like this to me before, and no one could have said this to me before: In any other medium, these words would be, literally, unspeakable. The guy couldn't have said this to me on the phone, because I would have hung up and not answered if the phone rang again, and he couldn't have said it to my face, because I wouldn't have let him finish. . . . I suppose the guy could have written me a nasty letter: He probably wouldn't have used the word "rectum," though, and he probably wouldn't have mailed the letter; he would have thought twice while he was addressing the envelope. But the nature of E-mail is that you don't think twice. You write and send.[54]

Permanence   Common decency aside, the risk of hostile e-messages—or any inappropriate mediated messages—is their permanence. It can be bad enough to blurt out a private thought or lash out in person, but at least there is no permanent record of your indiscretion. By contrast, a regrettable text message, e-mail, or web posting can be archived virtually forever. Even worse, it can be retrieved and forwarded in ways that can only be imagined in your worst dreams. The best advice, then, is to take the same approach with mediated messages that you do in person: Think twice before saying something you may later regret.

Choosing the Best Medium   A generation ago, choosing which communication medium to use wasn't very complicated: If a face-to-face conversation wasn't desirable or possible, you either wrote a letter or used the telephone. Today's communicators have many more options. If you want to put your thoughts in writing, you can use e-mail, text messaging, instant messaging . . . or the traditional pen-and-paper approach. If you want to speak, you can either use a "landline" telephone, a cell phone, or an Internet-based system.

TABLE 1-1   Factors to consider when choosing a communication channel

	Time Required for Feedback	Amount of Information Conveyed	Sender's Control Over How Message Is Composed	Control Over Receiver's Attention	Effectiveness for Detailed Messages
Face-to-face	Immediate (after contact established)	Highest	Moderate	Highest	Weak
Telephone	Immediate (after contact established)	Vocal, but not visual	Moderate	Less than in face-to-face setting	Weakest
Voice mail	Delayed	Vocal, but not visual	Higher (since receiver can't interrupt)	Low	Weak
E-mail	Delayed	Lowest (text only, no formatting)	High	Low	Better
Instant messaging	Immediate	Lowest (text only, no formatting)	High	Modest	Weak
Hard copy (e.g., handwritten or typed message)	Delayed	Words, numbers, and images, but no nonverbal cues	Highest	Low	Good

Adapted from R. B. Adler and J. M. Elmhorst, *Communicating at Work: Principles and Practices for Business and the Professions,* 9th ed. (New York: McGraw-Hill, 2008), p. 31.

Sometimes the choice of a medium is a no-brainer. If a friend says "phone me while I'm on the road," you know what to do. If your boss or professor only responds to e-mails, then it would be foolish to use any other approach. But in many other situations, you have several options available. Table 1-1 outlines the advantages and drawbacks of the most common ones. Choosing the best channel can make a real difference in your success. In one survey, managers who were identified as most "media sensitive" were almost twice as likely as their less savvy peers to receive top ratings in performance reviews.[55]

CULTURAL IDIOM

no-brainer:
requiring little thought or effort to understand or do

Clarifying Misconceptions About Communication

Having spent time talking about what communication is, we ought to also identify some things it is not.[56] Recognizing some misconceptions is important, not only because they ought to be avoided by anyone knowledgeable about the subject, but also because following them can get you into trouble.

Communication Does Not Always Require Complete Understanding

Most people operate on the implicit but flawed assumption that the goal of all communication is to maximize understanding between communicators. Although some understanding is necessary for us to comprehend one another's thoughts, there are some types of communication in which understanding as we usually conceive it isn't the primary goal.[57] Consider, for example:

- *Social rituals.* "How's it going?" you ask. "Great," the other person replies. The primary goal in exchanges like these is mutual acknowledgment: There's obviously no serious attempt to exchange information.

- *Many attempts to influence others.* A quick analysis of most television commercials shows that they are aimed at persuading viewers to buy products, not to understand the content of the commercial. In the same way, many of our attempts at persuading another to act as we want don't involve a desire to get the other person to understand what we want—just to comply with our wishes.

- *Deliberate ambiguity and deception.* When you decline an unwanted invitation by saying "I can't make it," you probably want to create the impression that the decision is really beyond your control. (If your goal was to be perfectly clear, you might say, "I don't want to get together. In fact, I'd rather do almost anything than accept your invitation.") As Chapters 3 and 6 explain in detail, we often equivocate precisely because we want to obscure our true thoughts and feelings.

- *Coordinated action.* Examples are conversations where satisfaction doesn't depend on full understanding. The term **coordination** has been used to describe situations in which participants interact smoothly, with a high degree of satisfaction but without necessarily understanding one another well.[58] Coordination without understanding can be satisfying in far more important situations. Consider the words "I love you." This is a phrase that can have many meanings: Among other things, it can mean "I admire you," "I feel great affection for you," "I desire you," "I am grateful to you," "I feel guilty," "I want you to be faithful to me," or even "I hope *you* love *me*."[59] It's not hard to picture a situation in which partners gain great satisfaction—even over a lifetime—without completely understanding that the mutual love they profess actually is quite different for each of them. The cartoon on page 25 reflects the fact that better understanding can sometimes lead to *less* satisfaction. "You mean you mostly love me because I've been there for you? Hey, a *dog* is there for you!"

Communication Will Not Solve All Problems

"If I could just communicate better . . ." is the sad refrain of many unhappy people who believe that if they could just express themselves better, their relationships would improve. Though this is sometimes true, it's an exaggeration to say that communicating—even communicating clearly—is a guaranteed panacea.

Communication Isn't Always a Good Thing

For most people, belief in the value of communication rates somewhere close to parenthood in their hierarchy of important values. In truth, communication is neither good nor bad in itself. Rather, its value comes from the way it is used. In this sense, communication is similar to fire: Flames in the fireplace on a cold night keep you warm and create a cozy atmosphere, but the same flames can kill if they spread into the room. Communication can be a tool for expressing warm feelings and useful facts, but under different circumstances the same words and actions can cause both physical and emotional pain.

"My wife understands me."

Meanings Rest in People, Not Words

It's a mistake to think that, just because you use a word in one way, others will do so, too.[60] Sometimes differing interpretations of symbols are easily caught, as when we might first take the statement "He's loaded" to mean the subject has had too much to drink, only to find out that he is quite wealthy. In other cases, however, the ambiguity of words and nonverbal behaviors isn't so apparent, and thus has more far-reaching consequences. Remember, for instance, a time when someone said to you, "I'll be honest," and only later did you learn that those words hid precisely the opposite fact. In Chapter 3 you'll read a great deal more about the problems that come from mistakenly assuming that meanings rest in words.

Communication Is Not Simple

Most people assume that communication is an aptitude that people develop without the need for training—rather like breathing. After all, we've been swapping ideas with one another since early childhood, and there are lots of people who communicate pretty well without ever having had a class on the subject. Though this picture of communication as a natural ability seems accurate, it's actually a gross oversimplification.[61]

Many people do learn to communicate skillfully because they have been exposed to models of such behavior by those around them. This principle of modeling explains why children who grow up in homes with stable relationships between family members have a greater chance of developing such relationships themselves. But even the best communicators aren't perfect: They often suffer the frustration of being unable to get a message across effectively, and they frequently misunderstand others. Furthermore, even the most successful people you know probably can identify ways in which their relationships could profit from better communication. These facts show that communication skills are rather like athletic ability: Even the most inept of us can learn to be more effective with training and practice, and those who are talented can always become better.

"I'm so glad we had this little talk, Earl!"

More Communication Isn't Always Better

Although it's certainly true that not communicating enough is a mistake, there are also situations when *too much* communication is a mistake. Sometimes excessive communication simply is unproductive, as when we "talk a problem to death," going over the same ground again and again without making any headway. And there are times when communicating too much can actually aggravate a problem. We've all had the experience of "talking ourselves into a hole"—making a bad situation worse by pursuing it too far. As McCroskey and Wheeless put it, "More and more negative communication merely leads to more and more negative results."[62]

There are even times when *no* communication is the best course. Any good salesperson will tell you that it's often best to stop talking and let the customer think about the product. And when two people are angry and hurt, they may say things they don't mean and will later regret. At times like these it's probably best to spend a little time cooling off, thinking about what to say and how to say it.

One key to successful communication, then, is to share an *adequate* amount of information in a *skillful* manner. Teaching you how to decide what information is adequate and what constitutes skillful behavior is one major goal of this book.

ETHICAL CHALLENGE

● **To Communicate or Not to Communicate?**

The explanations on pages 23–26 make it clear that communication is not a panacea. Explaining yourself and understanding others will not solve all problems; in fact, sometimes more communication leads to more problems. Think of an occasion (real or hypothetical) where more interaction would make matters worse. Imagine that the other person (or people) involved in this situation is (are) urging you to keep the channels of communication open. You know that if you do communicate more the situation will deteriorate, yet you don't want to appear uncooperative. What should you do?

Summary

This chapter began by defining *communication* as it will be examined in *Understanding Human Communication:* the process of creating meaning through symbolic interaction.

It introduced several communication contexts that will be covered in the rest of the book: intrapersonal, dyadic, small group, and public. The chapter also identified several types of needs that communication satisfies: physical, identity, social, and practical.

A linear and a transactional communication model were developed, demonstrating the superiority of the transactional model in representing the process-oriented nature of human interaction.

The chapter went on to explore the difference between effective and ineffective exchanges by discussing communication competence, showing that there is no single correct way to behave, that competence is situational and relational in nature, and that it can be learned. Competent communicators were described as being able to choose and perform appropriately from a wide range of behaviors, as well as being cognitively complex self-monitors who can take the perspective of others and who have commitment to important relationships. You also read that intercultural encounters often require extra levels of competence, and that mediated communication presents its own set of challenges.

After spending most of the chapter talking about what communication is, the chapter concluded by discussing what it is not by refuting several common misconceptions. It demonstrated that communication doesn't always require complete understanding and that it is not always a good thing that will solve every problem. It showed that more communication is not always better; that meanings are in people, not in words; and that communication is neither simple nor easy.

Key Terms

channel 9
communication 2
communication
    competence 13
coordination 24
decode 9
disinhibition 22
dyad 5
dyadic communication 5
encode 9
environment 10
feedback 10
interpersonal
    communication 5
intrapersonal
    communication 4

linear communication
    model 9
mass communication 6
mediated communication 9
message 29
mindfulness 20
noise 9
public communication 5
receiver 9
richness 21
sender 9
small group
    communication 5
symbol 3
transactional com-
    munication model 10

Activities

1. **Analyzing Your Communication Behavior** Prove for yourself that communication is both frequent and important by observing your interactions for a one-day period. Record every occasion in which you are involved in some sort of communication as it is defined on pages 2–8. Based on your findings, answer the following questions:

   1. What percentage of your waking day is involved in communication?

   2. What percentage of time do you spend communicating in the following contexts: intrapersonal, dyadic, small group, and public?

   3. What percentage of your communication is devoted to satisfying each of the following types of needs: physical, identity, social, and practical? (Note that you might try to satisfy more than one type at a time.)

Based on your analysis, describe five to ten ways you would like to communicate more effectively. For each item on your list of goals, describe who is involved (e.g., "my boss," "people I meet at parties") and how you would like to communicate differently (e.g., "act less defensively when criticized," "speak up more instead of waiting for them to approach me"). Use this list to focus your studies as you read the remainder of this book.

2. **Choosing the Most Effective Communication Channel** Decide which communication channel would be most effective in each of the following situations. Be prepared to explain your answer.

1. In class, an instructor criticizes you for copying work from other sources, but the work really was your own. You are furious, and you don't intend to accept the attack without responding. Which approach(es) would be best for you to use?

   a. Send your instructor an e-mail or write a letter explaining your objections.

   b. Telephone your instructor and explain your position.

   c. Schedule a personal meeting with your instructor.

2. You want to see whether the members of your extended family are able to view the photos you've posted on your family website. How can you find out how easily they can access the website?

   a. Demonstrate the website at an upcoming family get-together.

   b. Send them a link to the website as part of an e-mail.

   c. Phone family members and ask them about their ability to access websites.

3. You want to be sure the members of your office team are able to use the new voice mail system. Should you

   a. Send each employee an instruction manual for the system?

   b. Ask employees to send you e-mails or memos with any questions about the system?

   c. Conduct one or more training sessions where employees can try out the system and you can clear up any questions?

4. You've just been given two free tickets to tomorrow night's concert. How can you best find out whether your friend can go with you?

   a. Send her an e-mail and ask for a quick reply.

   b. Leave a message on your friend's answering machine asking her to phone you back.

   c. Send an instant message via your computer.

3. **Increasing Your Communicative Competence** Prove for yourself that communication competence can be increased by following these steps.

1. Identify a situation in which you are dissatisfied with your present communication skill.

2. Identify at least three distinct, potentially successful approaches you might take in this situation that are different from the one you have taken in the past. If you are at a loss for alternatives, consider how other people you have observed (both real and fictional characters) have handled similar situations.

3. From these three alternatives, choose the one you think would work best for you.

4. Consider how you could become more skillful at performing your chosen approach. For example, you might rehearse it alone or with friends, or you might gain pointers from watching others.

5. Consider how to get feedback on how well you perform your new approach. For instance, you might ask friends to watch you. In some cases, you might even be able to ask the people involved how you did.

This systematic approach to increasing your communicative competence isn't the only way to change, but it is one way to take the initiative in communicating more effectively.

For Further Exploration

For more resources about the nature of communication, see the *Understanding Human Communication* website at www.oup.com/us/uhc10. There you will find a variety of resources: a list of books and articles, links to descriptions of feature films and television shows at the *Now Playing* website, study aids, and a self-test to check your understanding of the material in this chapter.

CHAPTER HIGHLIGHTS

Communication depends on the way we perceive ourselves. You will appreciate the importance of the self as you read about:

- How communication shapes the self-concept
- The way culture shapes our self-perceptions
- The role of personality in shaping our perceptions
- How self-fulfilling prophecies can lead to either more satisfying or less productive communication

Our perceptions of others shape the way we communicate with them. Several factors influence these perceptions:

- Our success at constructing shared narratives through communication
- Our tendency to make several perceptual errors
- Factors arising from our own experience and from our prior relationship with that person
- Our cultural background
- Our ability to empathize

The skill of perception checking can help clarify mistaken perceptions, leading to a shared narrative and smoother communication.

To understand how this principle of identity management operates, Chapter 2 explains:

- The difference between perceived and presenting selves
- How we communicate to manage our identities, via both face to face and mediated channels
- Reasons why we communicate to manage our identities

The Self, Perception, and Communication

After studying the material in this chapter ...

You should understand:

1. The communicative influences that shape the self-concept.
2. How self-fulfilling prophecies influence behavior.
3. How perceptual tendencies and situational factors influence perception.
4. The influence of culture on perception and the self-concept.
5. The importance of empathy in communication.
6. How the process of identity management can result in presentation of multiple selves.
7. The reasons for and the ethical dimensions of identity management.

You should be able to:

1. Identify the ways you influence the self-concepts of others and the ways significant others influence your self-concept.
2. Identify the communication-related self-fulfilling prophecies that you have imposed on yourself, that others have imposed on you, and that you have imposed on others.
3. Identify how the perceptual tendencies described in this chapter have led you to develop distorted perceptions of yourself and others.
4. Use perception checking and empathy to be more accurate in your perceptions of others' behavior.
5. Describe the various identities you attempt to create and the ethical merit of your identity management strategies.

CULTURAL IDIOM
botched:
destroyed, ruined

- In biology class, a shy but earnest student mistakenly uses the term *orgasm* instead of *organism* when answering the professor's question. The entire class breaks into raucous laughter. The student remains quiet for the remainder of the semester.
- Despite her nervousness, a graduating student does her best to look and sound confident in a job interview. Although she leaves the session convinced she botched a big chance, a few days later she is surprised to receive a job offer.
- Two classmates, one black and the other white, are discussing their latest reading assignment in an American history class. "Malcolm X was quite a guy," the white student says sincerely to the black one. "You must be very proud of him." The black student is offended at what sounds like a condescending remark.
- A student is practicing his first speech for a public address class with several friends. "This is a stupid topic," he laments. The others assure him that the topic is interesting and that the speech sounds good. Later in class he becomes flustered because he believes that his speech is awful—and that belief affects his performance. As a result of his unenthusiastic delivery, the student receives a low grade on the assignment.

Stories like these probably sound familiar. Yet behind this familiarity lie principles that affect our communication more than almost any others discussed in this book.

- The messages we send can shape others' self-concepts and thus influence their communication.
- The image we present to the world varies from one situation to another.
- Two or more people often perceive the world in radically different ways, which presents major challenges for successful communicating.
- The beliefs each of us holds about ourselves—our self-concept—have a powerful effect on our own communication behavior.

These simple truths play a role in virtually all the important messages we send and receive. The goal of this chapter is to demonstrate the significance of these truths by describing how the ways in which we perceive ourselves and others shape our communication.

Communication and the Self

Nothing is more fundamental to understanding how we communicate than our sense of self. For that reason, the following pages introduce the notion of self-concept and explain how the way we view ourselves shapes our interaction with others.

Self-Concept Defined

The **self-concept** is a set of relatively stable perceptions that each of us holds about ourself. The self-concept includes our conception of what is unique about us and what makes us both similar to and different from others. To put it differently, the self-concept is rather like a mental mirror that reflects how we view ourselves: not only physical features, but also emotional states, talents, likes and dislikes, values, and roles.

We will have more to say about the nature of the self-concept shortly, but first you will find it valuable to gain a personal understanding of how this theoretical construct applies to you. You can do so by answering a simple question: "Who are you?"

A man or woman? What is your age? Your religion? Occupation?

There are many ways of identifying yourself. Take a few more minutes and list as many ways as you can to identify who you are. You'll need this list later in this chapter, so be sure to complete it now. Try to include all the characteristics that describe you, including

- Your moods or feelings
- Your appearance and physical condition
- Your social traits
- Talents you possess or lack
- Your intellectual capacity
- Your belief systems (religion, philosophy)
- Your strong beliefs
- Your social roles

Even a list of twenty or thirty terms would be only a partial description. To make this written self-portrait complete, your list would have to be hundreds—or even thousands—of words long.

Of course, not all items on such a list would be equally important. For example, the most significant part of one person's self-concept might consist of social roles, whereas for another it might consist of physical appearance, health, friendships, accomplishments, or skills.

An important element of the self-concept is **self-esteem:** our evaluations of self-worth. One person's self-concept might include being religious, tall, or athletic. That person's self-esteem would be shaped by how he or she felt about these qualities: "I'm glad that I am athletic," or "I am embarrassed about being so tall," for example.

Self-esteem has a powerful effect on the way we communicate.[1] People with high self-esteem are more willing to communicate than people with low self-esteem. They are more likely to think highly of others and expect to be accepted by others. They aren't afraid of others' reactions and perform well when others are watching them. They work harder for people who demand high standards of performance, and they are comfortable with others whom they view as superior in some way. When confronted with critical comments, they are comfortable defending themselves. By contrast, people with low self-esteem are likely to be critical of others and expect rejection from them. They are also critical of their own performances. They are sensitive to possible disapproval of others and perform poorly when being watched. They work harder for undemanding, less critical people. They feel threatened by people they view as superior in some way and have difficulty defending themselves against others' negative comments.

Communication and Development of the Self

So far we've talked about what the self-concept is, but at this point you may be asking what it has to do with the study of human communication. We can begin to answer this question by looking at how you came to possess your own self-concept.

Our identity comes almost exclusively from communication with others. As psychologists Arthur Combs and Donald Snygg put it:

> The self is essentially a social product arising out of experience with people. . . . We learn the most significant and fundamental facts about ourselves from . . . "reflected appraisals," inferences about ourselves made as a consequence of the ways we perceive others behaving toward us.[2]

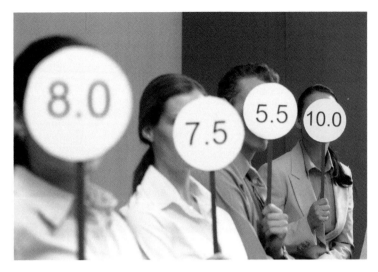

The term **reflected appraisal,** coined by Harry Stack Sullivan,[3] is a good one, because it metaphorically describes the fact that we develop an image of ourselves from the way we think others view us. This notion of the "looking-glass self" was introduced in 1902 by Charles H. Cooley, who suggested that we put ourselves in the position of other people and then, in our mind's eye, view ourselves as we imagine they see us.[4]

As we learn to speak and understand language, verbal messages—both positive and negative—also contribute to the developing self-concept. These messages continue later in life, especially when they come from what social scientists term **significant others**—people whose opinions we especially value. A teacher from long ago, a special friend or relative, or perhaps a barely known acquaintance whom you respected can all leave an imprint on how you view yourself. To see the importance of significant others, ask yourself how you arrived at your opinion of you as a student, as a person attractive to the opposite sex, as a competent worker, and so on and you will see that these self-evaluations were probably influenced by the way others regarded you.

As we grow older, the influence of significant others is less powerful.[5] The evaluations of others still influence beliefs about the self in some areas, such as physical attractiveness and popularity. In other areas, however, the looking glass of the self-concept has become distorted, so that it shapes the input of others to make it conform with our existing beliefs. For example, if your self-concept includes the element "poor student," you might respond to a high grade by thinking "I was just lucky" or "The professor must be an easy grader."

You might argue that not every part of one's self-concept is shaped by others, insisting there are certain objective facts that are recognizable by self-observation. After

UNDERSTANDING DIVERSITY

Deafness and Identity[6]

The experience of Howard offers a dramatic example of how reference groups and reflected appraisal can shape identity. Every member of Howard's immediate family—parents, brother, aunts, and uncles—was deaf. He spent his entire early childhood around deaf people and in his preschool life accepted this way of being as the natural state of affairs.

Even as a young child, Howard knew about deafness. The American Sign Language sign for "deaf" was part of his everyday vocabulary. But when he began school, Howard soon discovered that the same sign had a subtle but dramatically different meaning. Among his family, "deaf" meant "us—people who behave as expected." But in a mostly hearing world, the same term meant "a remarkable condition—different from normal."

This sense of difference can shape the identity of a deaf child, especially in environments where sign language is discouraged in favor of communication forms that are favored in the hearing world, such as lip reading and speaking. In such an environment, it's not hard to imagine how the identity "I'm deaf" can come to mean "I'm different," and then "I'm deficient." Howard's physical condition didn't change when he began school, but his sense of himself shifted due to the reflected appraisal of his teachers and the broader reference groups he experienced in the hearing world.

all, nobody needs to tell you that you are taller than others, speak with an accent, can run quickly, and so on. These facts are obvious.

Though it's true that some features of the self are immediately apparent, the *significance* we attach to them—the rank we assign them in the hierarchy of our list and the interpretation we give them—depends greatly on the social environment. The interpretation of characteristics such as weight depends on the way people important to us regard them. Being anything less than trim and muscular is generally regarded as undesirable because others tell us that slenderness is an ideal. In one study, young women's perceptions of their bodies changed for the worse after watching just thirty minutes of televised images of the "ideal" female form.[7] Furthermore, these distorted self-images can lead to serious behavioral disorders such as depression, anorexia nervosa, bulimia, and other eating disorders. In cultures and societies where greater weight is considered beautiful, a Western supermodel would be considered unattractive. In the same way, the fact that one is single or married, solitary or sociable, aggressive or passive takes on meaning depending on the interpretation that society attaches to those traits. Thus, the importance of a given characteristic in your self-concept has as much to do with the significance that you and others attach to it as with the existence of the characteristic.

Culture and the Self-Concept

The challenges and opportunities that come from cultural diversity are becoming more apparent with every passing year. But the power of culture is far more basic and powerful than most people realize. Although we seldom recognize the fact, our whole notion of the self is shaped by the culture in which we have been reared.[8]

The most obvious feature of a culture is the language its members use. If you live in an environment where everyone speaks the same tongue, then language will have little noticeable impact. But when your primary language is not the majority one, or when it is not prestigious, the sense of being a member of what social scientists call the "out-group" is strong. At this point the speaker of a nondominant language can react in one of two ways: either to feel pressured to assimilate by speaking the "better" language, or to refuse to accede to the majority language and maintain loyalty to the ethnic language.[9] In either case, the impact of language on the self-concept is powerful.

CULTURAL IDIOM

tongue:
language

On one hand, the feeling is likely to be "I'm not as good as speakers of the native language," and on the other, the belief is "there's something unique and worth preserving in my language." A case study of Hispanic managers illustrates the dilemma of speaking a nondominant language.[10] The managers—employees in a predominantly Anglo organization—felt their "Mexican" identity threatened when they found that the road to advancement would be smoother if they deemphasized their Spanish and adopted a more colloquial English style of speaking.

Cultures affect the self-concept in more subtle ways, too. Most Western cultures are highly individualistic, whereas other cultures—most Asian ones, for example—are traditionally much more collective.[11] When asked to identify themselves, Americans, Canadians, Australians, and Europeans would probably respond by giving their first name, surname, street, town, and country. Many Asians do it the other way around.[12] If you ask Hindus for their identity, they will give you their caste and village as well as their name. The Sanskrit formula for identifying one's self begins with lineage and goes on to family and house and ends with one's personal name.[13]

These conventions for naming aren't just cultural curiosities: They reflect a very different way of viewing one's self.[14] In collective cultures a person gains identity by belonging to a group. This means that the degree of interdependence among members of the society and its subgroups is much higher. Feelings of pride and self-worth are likely to be shaped not only by what the individual does, but also by the behavior of other members of the community. This linkage to others explains the traditional Asian denial of self-importance—a strong contrast to the self-promotion that is common in individualistic Western cultures. In Chinese written language, for example, the pronoun "I" looks very similar to the word for "selfish."[15] Table 2-1 summarizes some differences between individualistic Western cultures and more collective Asian ones.

This sort of cultural difference isn't just an anthropological curiosity. It shows up in the level of comfort or anxiety that people feel when communicating. In societies where the need to conform is great, there is a higher degree of communication apprehension. For example, as a group, residents of China, Korea, and Japan exhibit significantly more anxiety about speaking out than do members of individualistic cultures such as the United States and Australia.[16] It's important to realize that different levels of communication apprehension don't mean that shyness is a "problem" in some

TABLE 2-1   The Self in Individualistic and Collectivistic Cultures

Individualistic Cultures	Collectivistic Cultures
Self is separate, unique individual; should be independent, self-sufficient	People belong to extended families or in-groups; "we" or group orientation
Individual should take care of self and immediate family	Person should take care of extended family before self
Many flexible group memberships; friends based on shared interests and activities	Emphasis on belonging to a very few permanent in-groups, which have a strong influence over the person
Reward for individual achievement and initiative; individual decisions encouraged; individual credit and blame assigned	Reward for contribution to group goals and well-being; cooperation with in-group members; group decisions valued; credit and blame shared
High value on autonomy, change, youth, individual security, equality	High value on duty, order, tradition, age, group security, status, hierarchy

Adapted by Sandra Sudweeks from H. C. Triandis, "Cross-cultural Studies of Individualism and Collectivism," in J. Berman, ed., *Nebraska Symposium on Motivation* 37 (Lincoln, NE: University of Nebraska Press, 1990), pp. 41–133, and E. T. Hall, *Beyond Culture* (Garden City, NY: Doubleday, 1976).

cultures. In fact, just the opposite is true: In these cultures, reticence is valued. When the goal is to *avoid* being the nail that sticks out, it's logical to feel nervous when you make yourself appear different by calling attention to yourself. A self-concept that includes "assertive" might make a Westerner feel proud, but in much of Asia it would more likely be cause for shame.

The difference between individualism and collectivism shows up in everyday interaction. Communication researcher Stella Ting-Toomey has developed a theory that explains cultural differences in important norms, such as honesty and directness.[17] She suggests that in individualistic Western cultures where there is a strong "I" orientation, the norm of speaking directly is honored, whereas in collectivistic cultures where the main desire is to build connections between the self and others, indirect approaches that maintain harmony are considered more desirable. "I gotta be me" could be the motto of a Westerner, but "If I hurt you, I hurt myself" is closer to the Asian way of thinking.

The Self-Concept and Communication with Others

So far we've focused on how the self-concept has been shaped by our interpretations of messages *from* our cultural environment and influential others. Now we will explore how the self-concept shapes the way we communicate *with* other people.

Figure 2-1 pictures the relationship between the self-concept and behavior. It illustrates how the self-concept both shapes much of our communication behavior and is shaped by it. We can begin to examine the process by considering the self-concept you bring to an event. Suppose, for example, that one element of your self-concept is "nervous with authority figures." That image probably comes from the evaluations of significant others in the past—perhaps teachers or former employers. If you view yourself as nervous with authority figures like these, you will probably behave in nervous ways when you encounter them in the future—in a teacher-student conference or a job interview. That nervous behavior is likely to influence how others view your personality, which in turn will shape how they respond to you—probably in ways that reinforce the self-concept you brought to the event. Finally, the responses of others

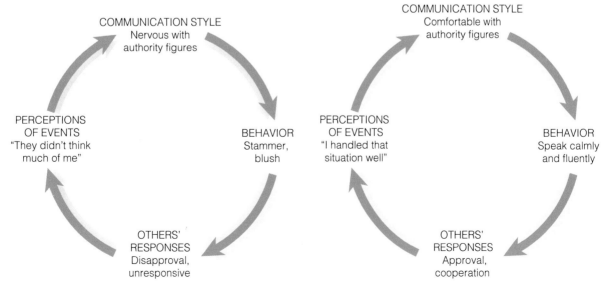

FIGURE 2-1   The Relationship Between the Self-Concept and Behavior

will affect the way you interpret future events: other job interviews, meetings with professors, and so on. This cycle illustrates how the chicken-and-egg nature of the self-concept, which is shaped by significant others in the past, helps to govern your present behavior, and influences the way others view you.

Not all communication behavior is driven by the self-concept. Some of our communication style is a function of our innate **personality**—a relatively consistent set of traits each of us exhibits across a variety of situations.[18] We use the notion of personality to characterize others as friendly or aloof, energetic or lazy, smart or stupid, and in literally thousands of other ways. In fact, one survey revealed almost eighteen thousand trait words in the English language that can be used to describe a personality.[19] People do seem to possess some innate personality traits. Psychologist Jerome Kagan reports that 10 percent of all children seem to be born with a biological disposition toward shyness.[20] Babies who stop playing when a stranger enters the room, for example, are more likely than others to be reticent and introverted as adolescents. Likewise, Kagan found that another 10 percent of children seem to be born with especially sociable dispositions. Research with twins also suggests that personality may be at least partially a matter of physical destiny.[21] Biologically identical twins are much more similar in sociability than are fraternal twins. These similarities are apparent not only in infancy but also when the twins have grown to adulthood, and are noticeable even when the twins have had different experiences.

The Self-Fulfilling Prophecy

The self-concept is such a powerful force on the personality that it not only determines how we communicate in the present, but also can actually influence our behavior and that of others in the future. Such occurrences come about through a phenomenon called the self-fulfilling prophecy.

A **self-fulfilling prophecy** occurs when a person's expectation of an outcome, and subsequent behavior, makes the outcome more likely to occur than would otherwise have been true. Self-fulfilling prophecies occur all the time although you might never have given them that label. For example, think of some instances you may have known:

- You expected to become nervous during a job interview, and your anxiety caused you to botch the session.

- You anticipated having a good (or terrible) time at a social affair, and your expectations led you to act in ways that shaped the outcome to fit your prediction.

- A teacher or boss explained a new task to you, saying that you probably wouldn't do well at first. You took these comments to heart, and as a result you didn't do well.

- A friend described someone you were about to meet, saying that you wouldn't like the person. Due in part to the prediction, you looked for—and found—reasons to dislike the new acquaintance.

In each of these cases, the outcome happened at least in part because it was predicted to occur. You needn't have botched the interview, the party might have been boring only because you helped make it so, you might have done better on the new task if your boss hadn't spoken up, and you might have liked the new acquaintance if your friend hadn't given you preconceptions. In other words, what helped make each outcome occur was the expectation that it would happen.

There are two types of self-fulfilling prophecies. The first type occurs when your own expectations influence your own behavior. Like the job interview and the party described earlier, there are many times when an outcome that need-n't have occurred does occur because you expect it to. In sports you have probably psyched yourself into playing either better or worse than usual, so that the only explanation for your unusual perfor-mance was your attitude that you would behave differently. The same principle operates for nervous public speakers: Communi-cators who feel anxious about facing an audience often create self-fulfilling prophecies about doing poorly that cause them to per-form less effectively.[22] (Chapter 12 offers advice on overcoming this kind of stage fright.)

Research has demonstrated the power of self-fulfilling prophe-cies. In one study, communicators who believed they were incom-petent proved less likely than others to pursue rewarding rela-tionships and more likely to sabotage their existing relationships than did people who were less critical of themselves.[23] On the other hand, students who perceived themselves as capable achieved more academically.[24] In another study, subjects who were sensitive to so-cial rejection tended to expect rejection, perceive it where it might not have existed, and overreact to their exaggerated perceptions in ways that jeopardized the quality of their relationships.[25] The self-fulfilling prophecy also operates on the job. For example, sales-people who perceive themselves as being effective communicators are more successful than those who perceive themselves as less ef-fective, despite the fact that there was no difference in the approach that members of each group used with customers. In other words, the apparent reason why some salespeople are successful is because they expect to succeed. As the nearby cartoon suggests, self-fulfilling prophecies can be physiologically induced: Researchers have found that putting a smile on your face, even if you're not in a good mood, can lead to a more positive disposition.[26]

A second category of self-fulfilling prophecies occurs when one person's expecta-tions govern another's actions.[27] The classic example was demonstrated by Robert Rosenthal and Lenore Jacobson in a study they described in their book *Pygmalion in the Classroom* (1968).[28] The experimenters told teachers that 20 percent of the children in a certain elementary school showed unusual potential for intellectual growth. The names of the 20 percent were drawn by means of a table of random numbers—much as if they were drawn out of a hat. Eight months later these unusual or "magic" chil-dren showed significantly greater gains in IQ than did the remaining children, who had not been singled out for the teachers' attention. The change in the teachers' be-havior toward these allegedly "special" children led to changes in the intellectual per-formance of these randomly selected children. Among other things, the teachers gave the "smart" students more time to answer questions, and provided more feedback to them. These children did better not because they were any more intelligent than their classmates, but because their teachers—significant others—communicated the ex-pectation that they could. In other words, it wasn't just what the teachers *believed* that made a difference; it was how these beliefs were conveyed by the teachers' *behavior*.

To put this phenomenon in context with the self-concept, we can say that when a teacher communicates to students the message "I think you're bright," they accept that evaluation and change their self-concepts to include that evaluation. Unfortunately, we can assume that the same principle holds for those students whose teachers send the message "I think you're stupid."

"*I don't sing because I am happy. I am happy because I sing.*"

CULTURAL IDIOM

psyched yourself:
affected your behavior by changing your thinking

CULTURAL IDIOM
in the same vein:
similarly

This type of self-fulfilling prophecy has been shown to be a powerful force for shaping the self-concept and thus the behavior of people in a wide range of settings outside of the schools. In medicine, patients who unknowingly receive placebos—substances such as injections of sterile water or doses of sugar pills that have no curative value—often respond just as favorably to treatment as do people who actually receive a drug. The patients believe they have taken a substance that will help them feel better, and this belief actually brings about a "cure." In psychotherapy, Rosenthal and Jacobson describe several studies that suggest that patients who believe they will benefit from treatment do so, regardless of the type of treatment they receive. In the same vein, when a doctor believes a patient will improve, the patient may do so precisely because of this expectation, whereas another person for whom the doctor has little hope often fails to recover. Apparently the patient's self-concept as sick or well—as shaped by the doctor—plays an important role in determining the actual state of health.

The self-fulfilling prophecy operates in families as well. If parents tell their children long enough that they can't do anything right, the children's self-concepts will soon incorporate this idea, and they will fail at many or most of the tasks they attempt. On the other hand, if children are told they are capable or lovable or kind persons, there is a much greater chance of their behaving accordingly.[29]

The self-fulfilling prophecy is an important force in communication, but it doesn't explain all behavior. There are certainly times when the expectation of an event's outcome won't bring about that outcome. Your hope of drawing an ace in a card game won't in any way affect the chance of that card turning up in an already shuffled deck, and your belief that good weather is coming won't stop the rain from falling. In the same way, believing you'll do well in a job interview when you're clearly not qualified for the position is unrealistic. Similarly, there will probably be people you don't like and occasions you won't enjoy, no matter what your attitude. To connect the self-fulfilling prophecy with the "power of positive thinking" is an oversimplification.

In other cases, your expectations will be borne out because you are a good predictor and not because of the self-fulfilling prophecy. For example, children are not equally well equipped to do well in school, and in such cases it would be wrong to say that a child's performance was shaped by a parent or teacher even though the behavior did match what was expected. In the same way, some workers excel and others fail, some patients recover and others don't—all according to our predictions but not because of them.

As we keep these qualifications in mind, it's important to recognize the tremendous influence that self-fulfilling prophecies play in our lives. To a great extent we are what we believe we are. In this sense we and those around us constantly create our self-concepts and thus ourselves.

CRITICAL THINKING PROBE

● **Self-Fulfilling Prophecies**

Explore how self-fulfilling prophecies affect your communication by answering the following questions:

1. Identify three communication-related predictions you make about others. What are the effects of these predictions? How would others behave differently if you did not impose these predictions?

2. Identify three self-fulfilling prophecies you impose on yourself. What are the effects of these prophecies? How would you communicate differently if you did not subscribe to them?

Perceiving Others

The first part of this chapter explored how our self-perceptions affect the way we communicate. The following pages examine how the ways we perceive others shape our interaction with them.

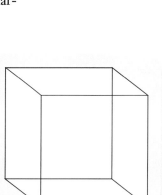

Steps in the Perception Process

In 1890 the famous psychologist William James described an infant's world as "one great blooming, buzzing confusion."[30] Babies—all humans, in fact—need some mechanisms to sort out the avalanche of stimuli that bombard us every moment. As you will read in the following pages, many of these stimuli involve others' behavior, and how we deal with those stimuli shapes our communication.

We sort out and make sense of others' behavior in three steps: selection, organization, and interpretation.

Selection Since we're exposed to more input than we can possibly manage, the first step in perception is the **selection** of which data we will attend to.

Some external factors help shape what we notice about others. For example, stimuli that are *intense* often attract our attention. Something that is louder, larger, or brighter stands out. This explains why—other things being equal—we're more likely to remember extremely tall or short people and why someone who laughs or talks loudly at a party attracts more attention (not always favorable) than do more quiet guests.

We also pay attention to *contrast* or *change* in stimulation. Put differently, unchanging people or things become less noticeable. This principle offers an explanation (excuse?) for why we take consistently wonderful people for granted when we interact with them frequently. It's only when they stop being so wonderful or go away that we appreciate them.

Along with external factors like intensity and contrast, *internal factors* shape how we make sense of others. For example, our *motives* often determine how we perceive people. Someone on the lookout for a romantic adventure will be especially aware of attractive potential partners, whereas the same person in an emergency might be oblivious to anyone but police or medical personnel.

Our *emotional state* also shapes what we select. For example, one study revealed that people in a happy mood were quick to notice when happy-appearing characters in a film appeared sadder, while unhappy subjects were quicker at noticing when sad characters appeared more happy.[31]

Organization After selecting information from the environment, we must arrange it in some meaningful way in order to make sense of the world. We call this stage **organization.**

The raw sense data we perceive can be organized in more than one way. The cube in Figure 2-2 illustrates this principle. If you look at the drawing long enough, you'll find that the faces of the cube change places. From one perspective you are looking down on the figure from above, but if you shift your point of view you will see it from beneath.

We organize our perceptions of other people using *perceptual schema*, cognitive frameworks that allow us to give order to the information we have selected.[32] Four types of schema help us classify others:

> *Physical constructs* classify people according to their appearance: beautiful or ugly, fat or thin, young or old, etc.

FIGURE 2-2 Cube

Role constructs use social position: student, attorney, wife, etc.

Interaction constructs focus on social behavior: friendly, helpful, aloof, sarcastic, etc.

Psychological constructs refer to internal states of mind and dispositions: confident, insecure, happy, neurotic, etc.

The kinds of constructs we use strongly affect the way we relate to others. For example, boys between eight and eleven years old tend to categorize peers according to their achievements, what they like and dislike, and personality, whereas girls in the same age range tend to perceive them according to their background and family.[33]

In cyberspace, where few nonverbal cues exist, it's harder to categorize people we haven't met in person. In text-based situations, strangers often rely on text-based cues to form impressions of others. In one study, for example, students relied on screen names to form impressions of strangers.[34] Experimenters asked college students to form impressions of fictional characters with names like "packerfan4" and "stinkybug." Using just the screen names, most of the respondents assigned attributes including biological sex, ethnicity, and age to the supposed owners of these names.

What constructs do you use to classify the people you encounter in your life? Consider how your relationships might change if you used different schema.

Once we have an organizing scheme to classify people, we use that scheme to make generalizations about members of the groups who fit our categories. For example, if you are especially aware of a person's sex, you might be alert to the differences between the way men and women behave or the way they are treated. If religion plays an important part in your life, you might think of members of your faith differently than you do others. If ethnicity is an important issue for you, you probably tune into the differences between members of various ethnic groups. There's nothing wrong with generalizations about groups as long as they are accurate. In fact, it would be impossible to get through life without them. But faulty overgeneralizations can lead to problems of stereotyping, which you'll read a few pages later.

Interpretation   Once we have selected and organized our perceptions, we interpret them in a way that makes some sort of sense. **Interpretation** plays a role in virtually every type of communication. Is the person who smiles at you across a crowded room interested in romance or simply being polite? Is a friend's kidding a sign of affection or irritation? Should you take an invitation to "drop by any time" literally or not?

There are several factors that cause us to interpret a person's behavior in one way or another. The first is our *degree of involvement* with the person. For example, research suggests that we tend to view people with whom we have or seek a relationship more favorably than those whom we observe from a detached perspective.[35]

Relational satisfaction is a second factor that influences our interpretation. The behavior that seems positive when you are happy with a partner might seem completely different when the relationship isn't satisfying. For example, couples in unsatisfying relationships are more likely than satisfied partners to blame one another when things go wrong.[36]

A third factor that influences interpretations is *personal experience*. What meanings have similar events held? For instance, if you've been gouged by landlords in the past, you might be skeptical about an apartment manager's assurances that careful housekeeping will ensure the refund of your cleaning deposit.

Assumptions about human behavior also influence interpretations. Do you assume people are lazy, dislike work, avoid responsibility, and must be coerced to do things, or do you believe people exercise self-direction and self-control, possess creativity, and seek

CULTURAL IDIOM
been gouged by:
was charged an excessive amount

responsibility? Imagine the differences in a boss who assumes workers fit the first description versus one who assumes they fit the second.

Expectations are another factor that shape our interpretations. When we anticipate people will behave in certain ways, our expectations color the way we interpret their behavior. For instance, if you go into a conversation expecting a hostile attitude, you're likely to hear a negative tone in the other person's voice—even if that tone isn't there. We'll talk more about how expectations affect perception later in this chapter.

Knowledge of others affects the way we interpret their actions. For instance, if you know a friend has just been jilted by a lover or fired from a job, you'll interpret his or her aloof behavior differently than if you were unaware of what happened. If you know an instructor is rude to all students, then you won't be likely to take his or her remarks personally.

Although we have talked about selection, organization, and interpretation separately, the three phases of perception can occur in differing sequences. For example, a parent's or babysitter's past interpretation (such as "Jason is a troublemaker") can influence future selections (his behavior becomes especially noticeable) and the organization of events (when there's a fight, the assumption is that Jason started it). As with all communication, perception is an ongoing process in which it is hard to pin down beginnings and endings.

Narratives and Perception

We all have our own story of the world, and often our story is quite different from those of others. A family member or roommate might think your sense of humor is inappropriate, whereas you think you're quite clever. You might blame an unsatisfying class on the professor, who you think is a long-winded bore. On the other hand, the professor might characterize the students as superficial and lazy and blame the class environment on them. (The discussion of emotive language in Chapter 3 will talk about the sort of name calling embedded in the previous sentences.)

Social scientists call the personal stories that we and others create to make sense of our personal world **narratives.**[37] In a few pages we will look at how a tool called "perception checking" can help bridge the gap between different narratives. For now, though, the important point is that differing narratives can lead to problematic communication.

After they take hold, narratives offer a framework for explaining behavior and shaping future communication. One study of sense making in organizations illustrates how the process operates on the job.[38] Researchers located employees who had participated in office discussions about cases where a fellow worker had received "differential treatment" from management about matters such as time off, pay, or work assignments. The researchers then analyzed the conversations that employees held with fellow workers about the differential treatment. The analysis revealed that these conversations were the occasion in which workers created and reinforced the meaning of the employee's behavior and management's

"I know what you're thinking, but let me offer a competing narrative."

Source: © The New Yorker Collection 2004 Harry Bliss from cartoonbank.com. All Rights Reserved.

CULTURAL IDIOM
jibe:
agree

response. For example, consider the way workers made sense of Jane Doe's habit of taking late lunches. As Jane's coworkers discuss her behaviors, they might decide that her late lunches aren't fair—or they might agree that late lunches aren't a big deal. Either way, the coworker's narrative of office events *defines* those events. Once they are defined, coworkers tend to seek reinforcement for their perceptions by keeping a mental scorecard rating their fellow employees and management. ("Did you notice that Bob came in late again today?" "Did you notice that the boss chose Jane to go on that trip to New York?") Although most of us like to think we make judgments about others on our own, this research suggests that sense making is an *interactive* process. In other words, reality in the workplace and elsewhere isn't "out there"; rather, we create it with others through communication.

Research on long-term happy marriages demonstrates that shared narratives don't have to be accurate to be powerful.[39] Couples who report being happily married after fifty or more years seem to collude in a relational narrative that doesn't always jibe with the facts. They agree that they rarely have conflict, although objective analysis reveals that they have had their share of disagreements and challenges. Without overtly agreeing to do so, they choose to blame outside forces or unusual circumstances for problems instead of attributing responsibility to one another. They offer the most charitable interpretations of one another's behavior, believing that the spouse acts with good intentions when things don't go well. They seem willing to forgive, or even forget, transgressions. Examining this research, one scholar concludes:

> Should we conclude that happy couples have a poor grip on reality? Perhaps they do, but is the reality of one's marriage better known by outside onlookers than by the players themselves? The conclusion is evident. One key to a long happy marriage is to tell yourself and others that you have one and then to behave as though you do![40]

Common Perceptual Tendencies

Shared narratives may be desirable, but they can be hard to achieve. Some of the biggest problems that interfere with understanding and agreement arise from errors in what psychologists call *attribution*—the process of attaching meaning to behavior. We attribute meaning to both our own actions and the actions of others, but we often use different yardsticks. Research has uncovered several perceptual errors that can lead to inaccurate attributions—and to troublesome communication.[41] By becoming aware of these errors, we can guard against them and avoid unnecessary conflicts.

We Make Snap Judgments   Our ancestors often had to make quick judgments about whether strangers were likely to be dangerous, and there are still times when this ability can be a survival skill.[42] But there are many cases when judging others without enough knowledge or information can get us into trouble. If you've ever been written off by a potential employer in the first few minutes of an interview, or have been unfairly rebuffed by someone you just met, then you know the feeling. Snap judgments become particularly problematic when they are based on **stereotyping**—exaggerated beliefs associated with a categorizing system. Stereotypes based on "primitive categories" like race, sex, and age may be founded on a kernel of truth, but they go beyond the facts at hand and make claims that usually have no valid basis.[43]

Three characteristics distinguish stereotypes from reasonable generalizations:

- *Categorizing others on the basis of easily recognized but not necessarily significant characteristics.* For example, perhaps the first thing you notice about a person is his or her skin color—but that may not be nearly as significant as the person's intelligence or achievements.

CULTURAL IDIOM
yardsticks:
standards of comparison

- *Ascribing a set of characteristics to most or all members of a group.* For example, you might unfairly assume that all older people are doddering or that all men are insensitive to women's concerns.

- *Applying the generalization to a particular person.* Once you believe all old people are geezers and all men are jerks, it's a short step to considering a particular senior citizen as senile, or a particular man as a chauvinist pig.

By adulthood, we tend to engage in stereotyping frequently, effortlessly, and often unconsciously.[44] Once we create and hold stereotypes, we seek out isolated behaviors that support our inaccurate beliefs. For example, men and women in conflict with each other often remember only behaviors of the opposite sex that fit their stereotypes.[45] They then point to these behaviors—which might not be representative of how the other person typically behaves—as "evidence" to suit their stereotypical and inaccurate claims: "Look! There you go criticizing me again. Typical for a woman!"

Stereotypes can plague interracial communication.[46] For example, surveys of college student attitudes show that many blacks characterize whites as "demanding" and "manipulative," while many whites describe blacks as "loud" and "ostentatious." Many African-American women report having been raised with stereotypical characterizations of whites (e.g., "Most whites cannot be trusted").

One way to avoid the kinds of communication problems that come from excessive stereotyping is to "decategorize" others, giving yourself a chance to treat people as individuals instead of assuming that they possess the same characteristics as every other member of the group to which you assign them.

We Often Judge Ourselves More Charitably Than We Judge Others   In an attempt to convince ourselves and others that the positive face we show to the world is true, we tend to judge ourselves in the most generous terms possible. Social scientists have labeled this tendency the **self-serving bias.**[47] When others suffer, we often blame the problem on their personal qualities. On the other hand, when we suffer, we find explanations outside ourselves. Consider a few examples:

- When they botch a job, we might think they weren't listening well or trying hard enough; when we botch a job, the problem was unclear directions or not enough time.

- When he lashes out angrily, we say he's being moody or too sensitive; when we blow off steam, it's because of the pressure we've been under.

- When she gets caught speeding, we say she should have been more careful; when we get caught, we deny we were driving too fast or we say, "Everybody does it."

The egocentric tendency to rate ourselves more favorably than others see us has been demonstrated experimentally.[48] In one study, members of a random sample of men were asked to rank themselves on their ability to get along with others.[49] Defying mathematical laws, all subjects—every last one—put themselves in the top half of the population. Sixty percent rated themselves in the top 10 percent of the population, and an amazing 25 percent believed they were in the top 1 percent. In the same study, 70 percent of the men ranked their leadership in the top 25 percent of the population, whereas only 2 percent thought they were below average. Sixty percent said they were in the top 25 percent in athletic abilities, whereas only 6 percent viewed themselves as below average.

Evidence like this suggests how uncharitable attitudes toward others can affect communication. Your harsh opinions of others can lead to judgmental messages, and

CULTURAL IDIOM

lashes out:
attacks with words

blow off steam:
release excess energy or anger

self-serving defenses of your own actions can result in a defensive response when others question your behavior.

We Pay More Attention to Negative Impressions Than Positive Ones   What do you think about Harvey? He's handsome, hardworking, intelligent, and honest. He's also very conceited.

Did the last quality mentioned make a difference in your evaluation? If it did, you're not alone. Research shows that when people are aware of both the positive and negative traits of another, they tend to be more influenced by the negative traits. In one study, for example, researchers found that job interviewers were likely to reject candidates who revealed negative information even when the total amount of information was highly positive.[50]

Sometimes this attitude makes sense. If the negative quality clearly outweighs any positive ones, you'd be foolish to ignore it. A surgeon with shaky hands and a teacher who hates children, for example, would be unsuitable for their jobs whatever their other virtues. But much of the time it's a bad idea to pay excessive attention to negative qualities and overlook positive ones. This is the mistake some people make when screening potential friends or dates. They find some who are too outgoing or too reserved, others who aren't intelligent enough, and still others who have the wrong sense of humor. Of course, it's important to find people you truly enjoy, but expecting perfection can lead to much unnecessary loneliness.

We Are Influenced by What Is Most Obvious   Every time we encounter another person, we are bombarded with more information than we can possibly manage. You can appreciate this by spending two or three minutes just reporting on what you can observe about another person through your five senses. ("Now I see you blinking your eyes . . . Now I notice you smiling . . . Now I hear you laugh and then sigh . . . Now I notice you're wearing a red shirt . . .") You will find that the list seems almost endless and that every time you seem to near the end, a new observation presents itself.

Faced with this tidal wave of sense data, we need to whittle down the amount of information we will use to make sense of others. There are three factors that cause us to notice some messages and ignore others. For example, we pay attention to stimuli that are *intense* (loud music, brightly dressed people), *repetitious* (dripping faucets, persistent people), or *contrastive* (a normally happy person who acts grumpy or vice versa). *Motives* also determine what information we select from our environment. If you're anxious about being late for a date, you'll notice whatever clocks may be around you; if you're hungry, you'll become aware of any restaurants, markets, and billboards advertising food in your path. Motives also determine how we perceive people.

If intense, repetitious, or contrastive information were the most important thing to know about others, there would be no problem. But the most noticeable behavior of others isn't always the most important. For example:

- When two children (or adults, for that matter) fight, it may be a mistake to blame the one who lashes out first. Perhaps the other one was at least equally responsible, by teasing or refusing to cooperate.

- You might complain about an acquaintance whose malicious gossiping or arguing has become a bother, forgetting that, by previously tolerating that kind of behavior, you have been at least partially responsible.

- You might blame an unhappy working situation on the boss, overlooking other factors beyond her control such as a change in the economy, the policy of higher management, or demands of customers or other workers.

We Cling to First Impressions, Even If Wrong Labeling people according to our first impressions is an inevitable part of the perception process. These labels are a way of making interpretations. "She seems cheerful." "He seems sincere." "They sound awfully conceited."

If they're accurate, impressions like these can be useful ways of deciding how to respond best to people in the future. Problems arise, however, when the labels we attach are inaccurate, because after we form an opinion of someone, we tend to hang on to it and make any conflicting information fit our image.

Suppose, for instance, you mention the name of your new

neighbor to a friend. "Oh, I know him," your friend replies. "He seems nice at first, but it's all an act." Perhaps this appraisal is off-base. The neighbor may have changed since your friend knew him, or perhaps your friend's judgment is simply unfair. Whether the judgment is accurate or not, after you accept your friend's evaluation, it will probably influence the way you respond to the neighbor. You'll look for examples of the insincerity you've heard about—and you'll probably find them. Even if the neighbor were a saint, you would be likely to interpret his behavior in ways that fit your expectations. "Sure he *seems* nice," you might think, "but it's probably just a front." As you read earlier in this chapter, this sort of suspicion can create a self-fulfilling prophecy, transforming a genuinely nice person into someone who truly becomes an undesirable neighbor as he reacts to your suspicious behavior.

The power of first impressions is important in personal relationships. A study of college roommates found that those who had positive initial impressions of each other were likely to have positive subsequent interactions, manage their conflicts constructively, and continue living together.[51] The converse was also true: Roommates who got off to a bad start tended to spiral negatively. This reinforces the wisdom and importance of the old adage, "You never get a second chance to make a first impression."

Given the almost unavoidable tendency to form first impressions, the best advice we can offer is to keep an open mind and be willing to change your opinion as events prove that the first impressions were mistaken.

We Tend to Assume That Others Are Similar to Us People commonly imagine that others possess the same attitudes and motives that they do. For example, research shows that people with low self-esteem imagine that others view them unfavorably, whereas people who like themselves imagine that others like them, too.[52] The frequently mistaken assumption that others' views are similar to our own applies in a wide range of situations. For example:

- You've heard a raunchy joke that you found funny. You might assume that it won't offend a somewhat conservative friend. It does.

CULTURAL IDIOM

off-base:
a mistake

a front:
a pretense

- You've been bothered by an instructor's tendency to get off the subject during lectures. If you were a professor, you'd want to know if anything you were doing was creating problems for your students, so you decide that your instructor will probably be grateful for some constructive criticism. Unfortunately, you're wrong.

- You lost your temper with a friend a week ago and said some things you regret. In fact, if someone said those things to you, you would consider the relationship finished. Imagining that your friend feels the same way, you avoid making contact. In fact, your friend feels that he was partly responsible and has avoided you because he thinks you're the one who wants to end things.

Examples like these show that others don't always think or feel the way we do and that assuming that similarities exist can lead to problems. For example, one study revealed that men evaluate women who initiate first dates as being more interested in sex than do the women who initiated the dates.[53]

How can you find out the other person's real position? Sometimes by asking directly, sometimes by checking with others, and sometimes by making an educated guess after you've thought the matter out. All these alternatives are better than simply assuming that everyone would react the way you do.

Don't misunderstand: We don't always commit the kind of perceptual errors described in this section. Sometimes, for instance, people *are* responsible for their misfortunes, and sometimes our problems are not our fault. Likewise, the most obvious interpretation of a situation may be the correct one. Nonetheless, a large amount of research has proved again and again that our perceptions of others are often distorted in the ways listed here. The moral, then, is clear: Don't assume that your first judgment of a person is accurate.

CRITICAL THINKING PROBE

● **Perceiving Others and Yourself**

1. You can gain appreciation for the way perceptual errors operate by making two attributions for each situation that follows: Develop your first explanation for the behavior as if you were the person involved. Your second explanation for the behavior should be developed as if someone you dislike were the person described.

   - Dozing off in class
   - Getting angry at a customer on the job
   - Dressing sloppily in public
   - Being insensitive to a friend's distress
   - Laughing at an inappropriate or offensive joke

2. If your explanations for these behaviors differ, ask yourself why. Are the differing attributions justifiable, or do they support the tendency to make the perceptual errors listed on pages 44–48?

3. How do these perceptual errors operate in making judgments about others' behavior, especially when those others come from different social groups?

Perception and Culture

Perceptual differences make communication challenging enough between members of the same culture. But when communicators come from different cultures, the potential for misunderstandings is even greater.

UNDERSTANDING DIVERSITY
Non-Western Views of Western Medical Care

Author Anne Fadiman explains why some Hmong refugees from the mountains of Laos preferred their traditional shamanistic healers, called txiv neebs, *to American doctors.*[54] *After the Hmong's objections are made explicit, it becomes clear why Western medicine can feel threatening and intrusive to patients who are already uncomfortable in a strange new environment.*

A *txiv neeb* might spend as much as eight hours in a sick person's home; doctors forced their patients, no matter how weak they were, to come to the hospital, and then might spend only twenty minutes at their bedsides. *Txiv neebs* were polite and never needed to ask questions; doctors asked many rude and intimate questions about patient's lives, right down to their sex-

ual and excretory habits. *Txiv neebs* could render an immediate diagnosis; doctors often demanded samples of blood (or even urine or feces, which they liked to keep in little bottles), took X rays, and waited for days for the results to come back from the laboratory—and then, after all that, sometimes they were unable to identify the cause of the problem. *Txiv neebs* never undressed their patients; doctors asked patients to take off all their clothes, and sometimes dared to put their fingers inside women's vaginas. *Txiv neebs* knew that to treat the body without treating the soul was an act of patent folly; doctors never even mentioned the soul.

Excerpt from "Do Doctors Eat Brains?" (*The Spirit Catches You and You Fall Down*).

Culture provides a perceptual filter that influences the way we interpret even the simplest events. This fact was demonstrated in studies exploring the domination of vision in one eye over the other.[55] Researchers used a binocularlike device that projects different images to each eye. The subjects were twelve Americans and twelve Mexicans. Each was presented with ten pairs of photographs, each pair containing one picture from U.S. culture (e.g., a baseball game) and one from Mexican culture (e.g., a bullfight). After viewing each pair of images, the subjects reported what they saw. The results clearly indicated the power of culture to influence perceptions: Subjects had a strong tendency to see the image from their own background.

The same principle causes people from different cultures to interpret similar events in different ways. Blinking while another person talks may be hardly noticeable to North Americans, but the same behavior is considered impolite in Taiwan. The beckoning finger motion that is familiar to Americans is an insulting gesture in most Middle and Far Eastern countries.

Even beliefs about the very value of talk differ from one culture to another.[56] North American culture views talk as desirable and uses it to achieve social purposes as well as to perform tasks. Silence in conversational situations has a negative value. It is likely to be interpreted as lack of interest, unwillingness to communicate, hostility, anxiety, shyness, or a sign of interpersonal incompatibility. Furthermore, the *kind* of talk that Westerners admire is characterized by straightforwardness and honesty. Being indirect or vague—"beating around the bush," it might be labeled—has a negative connotation.

On the other hand, most Asian cultures discourage the expression of thoughts and feelings. Silence is valued, as Taoist sayings indicate: "In

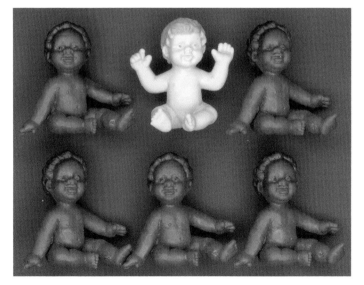

CULTURAL IDIOM

"save face":
protect one's dignity

come-on:
sexual advance

much talk there is great weariness," or "One who speaks does not know; one who knows does not speak." Unlike Westerners, who are uncomfortable with silence, Japanese and Chinese believe that remaining quiet is the proper state when there is nothing to be said. To Easterners, a talkative person is often considered a show-off or insincere. And when an Asian does speak up on social matters, the message is likely to be phrased indirectly to "save face" for the recipient.

It is easy to see how these different views of speech and silence can lead to communication problems when people from different cultures meet. Both the talkative Westerner and the silent Easterner are behaving in ways they believe are proper, yet each views the other with disapproval and mistrust. This may require them to recognize and deal with their **ethnocentrism**—the attitude that one's own culture is superior to others. An ethnocentric person thinks—either privately or openly—that anyone who does not belong to his or her in-group is somehow strange, wrong, or even inferior. Only when people recognize the different standards of behavior can they adapt to one another, or at least understand and respect their differences.

Perceptual differences are just as important right at home when members of different co-cultures interact. Failure to recognize co-cultural differences can lead to unfortunate and unnecessary misunderstandings. For example, an uninformed white teacher or police officer might interpret the downcast eyes of a Latino female as a sign of avoidance, or even dishonesty, when in fact this is the proper behavior in her culture for a female being addressed by an older man. To make direct eye contact in such a case would be considered undue brashness or even a sexual come-on.

Cross-cultural differences can be quite subtle. For example, one study revealed that, when meeting with academic counselors, Latinos preferred to be respected as members of their own culture as well as individuals. On the other hand, blacks preferred to be acknowledged as individuals rather than being identified as members of an ethnic group.[57]

Along with ethnicity, geography also can influence perception. A fascinating series of studies revealed that climate and geographic latitude were remarkably accurate predictors of communication predispositions.[58] People living in southern latitudes of the United States are more socially isolated, less tolerant of ambiguity, higher in self-esteem, more likely to touch others, and more likely to verbalize their thoughts and feelings. This sort of finding helps explain why communicators who travel from one part of a country to another find that their old patterns of communicating don't work as well in their new location. A southerner whose relatively talkative, high-touch style seemed completely normal at home might be viewed as pushy and aggressive in a new northern home.

Empathy and Perception

By now it is clear that differing perceptions present a major challenge to communicators. One solution is to increase the ability to empathize. **Empathy** is the ability to re-create another person's perspective, to experience the world from the other's point of view.

Dimensions of Empathy   As we'll use the term here, *empathy* has three dimensions.[59] On one level, empathy involves *perspective taking*—the ability to take on the viewpoint of another person. This understanding requires a suspension of judgment, so that for the moment you set aside your own opinions and take on those of the other person. Besides cognitive understanding, empathy also has an *emotional* dimension that allows us to experience the feelings that others have. We know their fear, joy, sadness, and so on. When we combine the perspective-taking and emotional dimensions, we

UNDERSTANDING DIVERSITY

Today's Lesson: Empathy

Time and time again, it was the bathroom stalls that got to Laura Manis and Kevin McCarthy.

"It's doable, but it's tight," said Manis, as she maneuvered a three-point turn into one stall.

"I should have come in forward," she observed after spending several minutes backing into another.

"I'm glad I didn't really have to go to the bathroom," said McCarthy after emerging from a third.

The pair, both second-year students in the University of Cincinnati's physical therapy assisting program, visited four suburban restaurants Thursday in an exercise that was part lesson in empathy and part consumer survey. Though neither has any physical disability, they and their classmates spent the day in wheelchairs to see how accessible 44 area restaurants were. Working off a checklist, 11 pairs of students tested the ramps, entrances, tables, salad bar, and bathrooms of establishments.

"Students come away with the impression that there are a lot of barriers and obstacles for (disabled) people if they want to lead a normal life," said Tina Whalen, the instructor who organized a similar exercise two years ago. "I think it's really an eye-opener, too, as far as an energy expenditure. By the time they get into a restaurant, through the door and up to a table, some of them are too tired to eat."

Recent legislation such as the 1990 Americans with Disabilities Act has made it illegal for businesses to discriminate on the basis of physical handicaps, and most buildings are now required to have wheelchair access and other provisions for the disabled. But Thursday, the students found that legal doesn't always mean easy—or safe. Take, for instance, the wheelchair ramp into the front door of Wendy's fast-food restaurant near Tri-County Mall. It slopes out of a pair of wide doors—and into the restaurant's drive-through lane.

McCarthy and Manis found the excursion a reinforcement of lessons learned in the classroom. "This [exercise] allows us the opportunity to experience the reality of life of someone who's disabled, as opposed to just learning about it in a textbook," said Manis.

Julie Irwin

see that empathizing allows us to experience the other's perception—in effect, to become that person temporarily. A third dimension of empathy is a genuine *concern* for the welfare of the other person. When we empathize we go beyond just thinking and feeling as others do and genuinely care about their well-being.

It is easy to confuse empathy with **sympathy,** but the concepts are different in two important ways. First, sympathy means you feel compassion *for* another person's predicament, whereas empathy means you have a personal sense of what that predicament is like. Consider the difference between sympathizing with an unwed mother or a homeless person and empathizing with them—imagining what it would be like to be in their position. Despite your concern, sympathy lacks the degree of identification that empathy entails. When you sympathize, it is the other's confusion, joy, or pain. When you empathize, the experience becomes your own, at least for the moment. Both perspectives are important ones, but empathy is clearly the more complete of the two.

Empathy is different from sympathy in a second way. We only sympathize when we accept the reasons for another's pain as valid, whereas it's possible to empathize without feeling sympathy. You can empathize with a difficult relative, a rude stranger, or even a criminal without feeling much sympathy for that person. Empathizing allows you to understand another person's motives without requiring you to agree with them. After empathizing, you will almost certainly understand a person better, but sympathy won't always follow.

"How would you feel if the mouse did that to you?"

The ability to empathize seems to exist in a rudimentary form in even the youngest children.[60] Virtually from birth, infants become visibly upset when they hear another infant crying, and children who are a few months old cry when they observe another child crying. Young children have trouble distinguishing others' distress from their own. If, for example, one child hurts his finger, another child might put her own finger in her mouth as if she were feeling pain. Researchers report cases in which children who see their parents crying wipe their own eyes, even though they are not crying.

Although infants and toddlers may have a basic capacity to empathize, studies with twins suggest that the degree to which we are born with the ability to sense how others are feeling varies according to genetic factors. Although some people may have an inborn edge, environmental experiences are the key to developing the ability to understand others. Specifically, the way in which parents communicate with their children seems to affect their ability to understand others' emotional states. When parents point out to children the distress that others feel from their misbehavior ("Look how sad Jessica is because you took her toy. Wouldn't you be sad if someone took away your toys?"), those children gain a greater appreciation that their acts have emotional consequences than they do when parents simply label behavior as inappropriate ("That was a mean thing to do!").

There is no consistent evidence that suggests that the ability to empathize is greater for one sex or the other.[61] Some people, however, seem to have a hereditary capacity for greater empathizing than do others.[62] Studies of identical and fraternal twins indicate that identical female twins are more similar to one another in their ability to empathize than are fraternal twins. Interestingly, there seems to be no difference between males. Although empathy may have a biological basis, environment can still play an important role. For example, parents who are sensitive to their children's feelings tend to have children who reach out to others.[63]

Total empathy is impossible to achieve. Completely understanding another person's point of view is simply too difficult a task for humans with different backgrounds and limited communication skills. Nonetheless, it is possible to get a strong sense of what the world looks like through another person's eyes.

A willingness to empathize can make a difference in everyday disputes. For example, communication researchers have spelled out how understanding opposing views can increase understanding and constructive problem solving in conflicts between environmentalists who want to preserve native species and landowners who want to earn a profit. After the parties begin to see one another's point of view, they can discover ways of protecting native species *and* allow landowners to carry on their enterprises.[64]

Cathy

Perception Checking   Good intentions and a strong effort to empathize are one way to understand others. Along with a positive attitude, however, there is a simple tool that can help you interpret the behavior of others more accurately. To see how this tool operates, consider how often others jump to mistaken conclusions about your thoughts, feelings, and motives:

"Why are you mad at me?" (Who said you were?)

"What's the matter with you?" (Who said anything was the matter?)

"Come on now. Tell the truth." (Who said you were lying?)

As you'll learn in Chapter 7, even if your interpretation is correct, a dogmatic, mind-reading statement is likely to generate defensiveness. The skill of **perception checking** provides a better way to handle your interpretations. A complete perception check has three parts:

- A description of the behavior you noticed;
- At least two possible interpretations of the behavior;
- A request for clarification about how to interpret the behavior.

Perception checks for the preceding three examples would look like this:

"When you stomped out of the room and slammed the door *[behavior]*, I wasn't sure whether you were mad at me *[first interpretation]* or just in a hurry *[second interpretation]*. How did you feel *[request for clarification]*?"

"You haven't laughed much in the last couple of days *[behavior]*. I wonder whether something's bothering you *[first interpretation]* or whether you're just feeling quiet *[second interpretation]*. What's up *[request for clarification]*?"

"You said you really liked the job I did *[behavior]*, but there was something about your voice that made me think you may not like it *[first interpretation]*. Maybe it's just my imagination, though *[second interpretation]*. How do you really feel *[request for clarification]*?"

Perception checking is a tool for helping us understand others accurately instead of assuming that our first interpretation is correct. Because its goal is mutual understanding, perception checking is a cooperative approach to communication. Besides leading to more accurate perceptions, it minimizes defensiveness by preserving the other person's face. Instead of saying in effect "I know what you're thinking . . ." a perception check takes the more respectful approach that states or implies "I know I'm not qualified to judge you without some help."

Sometimes a perception check won't need all of the parts listed earlier to be effective:

"You haven't dropped by lately. Is anything the matter *[single interpretation combined with request for clarification]*?"

"I can't tell whether you're kidding me about being cheap or if you're serious *[behavior combined with interpretations]*. Are you mad at me?"

"Are you *sure* you don't mind driving? I can use a ride if it's no trouble, but I don't want to take you out of your way *[no need to describe behavior]*."

Of course, a perception check can succeed only if your nonverbal behavior reflects the open-mindedness of your words. An accusing tone of voice or a hostile glare will contradict the sincerely worded request for clarification, suggesting that you have already made up your mind about the other person's intentions.

CULTURAL IDIOM

preserving the other person's face:
protecting the other's dignity

dropped by:
made an unplanned visit

CULTURAL IDIOM

turn the tables:
reverse the point of view

Communication and Identity Management

So far we have described how communication shapes the way communicators view themselves and others. In the remainder of this chapter we turn the tables and focus on **identity management**—the communication strategies people use to influence how others view them. In the following pages you will see that many of our messages aim at creating desired impressions.

Public and Private Selves

To understand why identity management exists, we have to discuss the notion of self in more detail. So far we have referred to the "self" as if each of us had only one identity. In truth, each of us possesses several selves, some private and others public. Often these selves are quite different.

The **perceived self** is a reflection of the self-concept. Your perceived self is the person you believe yourself to be in moments of honest self-examination. We can call the perceived self "private" because you are unlikely to reveal all of it to another person. You can verify the private nature of the perceived self by reviewing the self-concept list you developed while reading pages 32–33. You'll probably find some elements of yourself there that you would not disclose to many people, and some that you would not share with anyone. You might, for example, be reluctant to share some feelings about your appearance ("I think I'm rather unattractive"), your intelligence ("I'm not as smart as I wish I was"), your goals ("the most important thing to me is becoming rich"), or your motives ("I care more about myself than about others").

In contrast to the perceived self, the **presenting self** is a public image—the way we want to appear to others.

In most cases the presenting self we seek to create is a socially approved image: diligent student, loving partner, conscientious worker, loyal friend, and so on. Social norms often create a gap between the perceived and presenting selves. For instance, Table 2-2 shows that the self-concepts of the members of one group of male and female college students were quite similar, but that their public selves were different in several respects from both their private selves and the public selves of the opposite sex.[65]

"Hah! This is the Old King Cole nobody ever sees."

Sociologist Erving Goffman used the word **face** to describe the presenting self, and he coined the term **facework** to describe the verbal and nonverbal ways we act to maintain our own presenting image and the images of others.[66] He argued that each of us can be viewed as a kind of playwright, who creates roles that we want others to believe, as well as the performer who acts out those roles.

Facework involves two tasks: Managing our own identity and communicating in ways that reinforce the identities that others are trying to present.[67] You can see how these two goals operate by recalling a time when you've used self-deprecating humor to defuse a potentially unpleasant situation. Suppose, for example, that a friend gave you confusing directions to a party that caused you to be late. "Sorry I got lost," you might have said. "I'm a terrible navigator." This sort of mild self-putdown accomplishes two things at once: It preserves the other person's face by implicitly saying "It's not your fault." At the same time, your mild self-debasement shows that you're a nice person who doesn't find faults in others or make a big issue out of small problems.[68]

TABLE 2-2   Self-Selected Adjectives Describing Perceived and Presenting Selves of College Students

Perceived Self		Presenting Self	
Men	Women	Men	Women
1. Friendly	1. Friendly	1. Wild	1. Active
2. Active	2. Responsible	2. Able	2. Responsible
3. Responsible	3. Independent	3. Active	3. Able
4. Independent	4. Capable	4. Strong	4. Bright
5. Capable	5. Sensible	5. Proud	5. Warm
6. Polite	6. Active	6. Smart	6. Funny
7. Attractive	7. Happy	7. Brave	7. Independent
8. Smart	8. Curious	8. Capable	8. Proud
9. Happy	9. Faithful	9. Responsible	9. Sensible
10. Funny	10. Attractive	10. Rough	10. Smart

Adapted from C. M. Shaw and R. Edwards, "Self-Concepts and Self-Presentations of Males and Females: Similarities and Differences," *Communication Reports* 10 (1997): 55–62.

Characteristics of Identity Management

Now that you have a sense of what identity management is, we can look at some characteristics of this process.

We Strive to Construct Multiple Identities   In the course of even a single day, most people play a variety of roles: respectful student, joking friend, friendly neighbor, and helpful worker, to suggest just a few. We even play a variety of roles with the same person. As you grew up you almost certainly changed characters as you interacted with your parents. In one context you acted as the responsible adult ("You can trust me with the car!"), and in another context you were the helpless child ("I can't find my socks!"). At some times—perhaps on birthdays or holidays—you were a dedicated family member, and at other times you may have played the role of rebel. Likewise, in romantic relationships we switch among many ways of behaving, depending on the context: friend, lover, business partner, scolding critic, apologetic child, and so on.

The ability to construct multiple identities is one element of communication competence. For example, the style of speaking or even the language itself can reflect a choice about how to construct one's identity. We recall an African-American colleague who was also minister of a Southern Baptist congregation consisting mostly of black members. On campus his manner of speaking was typically professorial, but a visit to hear him preach one Sunday revealed a speaker whose style was much more animated and theatrical, reflecting his identity in that context. Likewise, one scholar pointed out that bilingual Latinos in the United States often choose whether to use English or Spanish depending on the kind of identity they are seeking in a given conversation.[69]

Identity Management Is Collaborative   As we perform like actors trying to create a front, our "audience" is made up of other actors who are trying to create their own characters. Identity-related communication is a kind of process theater in which we collaborate with other actors to improvise scenes in which our characters mesh.

You can appreciate the collaborative nature of identity management by thinking about how you might handle a gripe with a friend or family member who has failed to pass along a phone message that arrived while you were away from home. Suppose that you decide to raise the issue tactfully in an effort to avoid seeming like a nag (desired role for yourself: "nice person") and also to save the other person from the embarrassment of being confronted (hoping to avoid suggesting that the other person's role is "screw-up"). If your tactful bid is accepted, the dialogue might sound like this:

You: ". . . By the way, Jenny told me she called yesterday. If you wrote a note, I guess I missed seeing it."

Other: "Oh . . . sorry. I meant to write a note, but as soon as I hung up, the doorbell rang, and then I had to run off to class."

You: *(in friendly tone of voice)* "That's okay. I sure would appreciate from now on if you'd leave me a note."

Other: "No problem."

In this upbeat conversation, both you and the other person accepted one another's bids for identity as basically thoughtful people. As a result, the conversation ran smoothly. Imagine, though, how different the outcome would be if the other person didn't accept your role as "nice person":

You: ". . . By the way, Jenny told me she called yesterday. If you wrote a note, I guess I missed seeing it."

Other: *(defensively)* "Okay, so I forgot. It's not that big a deal. You're not perfect yourself, you know!"

Your first bid as "nice, face-saving person" was rejected. At this point you have the choice of persisting in trying to play the original role: "Hey, I'm not mad at you, and I know I'm not perfect!" Or, you might switch to the new role of "unjustly accused person," responding with aggravation "I never said I was perfect. But we're not talking about me here . . ."

As this example illustrates, *collaboration* doesn't mean the same thing as *agreement*.[70] The small issue of the phone message might mushroom into a fight in which you and the other person both adopt the role of combatants. The point here is that virtually all conversations provide an arena in which communicators construct their identities in response to the behavior of others. As you read in Chapter 1, communication isn't made up of discrete events that can be separated from one another. Instead, what happens at one moment is influenced by what each party brings to the interaction and by what happened in their relationship up to that point.

Identity Management Can Be Conscious or Unconscious   At this point you might object to the notion of strategic identity management, claiming that most of your communication is spontaneous and not a deliberate attempt to present yourself in a certain way. However, you might acknowledge that some of your communication involves a conscious attempt to manage impressions.

There's no doubt that sometimes we are highly aware of managing our identities. Most job interviews and first dates are clear examples of conscious identity management. But in other cases we unconsciously act in ways that are really small public performances.[71] For example, experimental subjects expressed facial disgust in reaction to eating sandwiches laced with a supersaturated saltwater solution only when there was another person present: When they were alone, they made no faces when eating the same sandwiches.[72] Another study showed that communicators engage in facial mimicry (such as smiling or looking sympathetic in response to another's message) in face-to-face settings only when their expressions can be seen by the other person. When they are speaking over the phone and their reactions cannot be seen, they do not make the same expressions.[73] Studies like these suggest that most of our behavior is aimed at sending messages to others—in other words, identity management.

The experimental subjects described in the last paragraph didn't consciously think, "Somebody is watching me eat this salty sandwich, so I'll make a face," or, "Since I'm in a face-to-face conversation I'll show I'm sympathetic by mimicking the facial expressions of my conversational partner." Reactions like these are often instantaneous and outside of our conscious awareness.

In the same way, many of our choices about how to act in the array of daily interactions aren't deliberate, strategic decisions. Rather, they rely on "scripts" that we have developed over time. You probably have a variety of roles for managing your identity from which to choose in familiar situations such as dealing with strangers, treating customers at work, interacting with family members, and so on. When you find yourself in familiar situations like these, you probably slip into these roles quite often. Only when those roles don't seem quite right do you deliberately construct an approach that reflects how you want the scene to play out.

Despite the claims of some theorists, it seems like an exaggeration to suggest that *all* behavior is aimed at managing identities. Young children certainly aren't strategic communicators. A baby spontaneously laughs when pleased, and cries when sad or uncomfortable, without any notion of creating an impression in others. Likewise, there are almost certainly times when we, as adults, act spontaneously. But when a significant other questions the self we try to present, the likelihood of acting to prop it up increases. This process isn't always conscious: At a nonconscious level of awareness we monitor others' reactions and swing into action when our face is threatened—especially by significant others.[74]

People Differ in Their Degree of Identity Management   Some people are much more aware of their identity management behavior than others. These high self-monitors have the ability to pay attention to their own behavior and others' reactions, adjusting their communication to create the desired impression. By contrast, low self-monitors express what they are thinking and feeling without much attention to the impression their behavior creates.[75]

There are certainly advantages to being a high self-monitor.[76] People who pay attention to themselves are generally good actors who can create the impression they want, acting interested when bored, or friendly when they really feel quite the opposite. This allows them to handle social situations smoothly, often putting others at ease. They are also good "people-readers" who can adjust their behavior to get the desired reaction from others. Along with these advantages, there are some potential disadvantages to being an extremely high self-monitor. The analytical nature of high self-monitors may prevent them from experiencing events completely, because a portion of their attention will always be viewing the situation from a detached position. High

CULTURAL IDIOM
"scripts":
practiced responses

to play out:
to proceed to a conclusion

MEDIA ROOM
The Challenges of Identity Management

Characters in films often communicate in ways that help craft the identity they want to present. As in real life, the stories described below illustrate both the benefits and costs of constructing identities that don't reflect our true nature.

The animated *Shark Tale* is an amusing illustration of characters who reap the benefits and suffer the consequences of presenting false identities. Oscar (Will Smith) is a fast-talking small fish who changes from nobody to celebrity when he is mistaken for a brazen "shark slayer." Given his newfound fame and happiness, it's not surprising that Oscar is willing to live a lie. Lenny (Jack Black) is a great white shark with a sensitive side and a secret about his identity: He's a vegetarian. When Lenny's secret is revealed, he becomes the object of scorn and ridicule. Both characters find themselves exhausted from managing their false identities and ultimately return to their true nature, which they learn is also preferred by those who love them most.

Brokeback Mountain is a more realistic and disturbing account of the dilemmas that can come from both disclosing and hiding our true identities. In 1963, Ennis Del Mar (Heath Ledger) and Jack Twist (Jake Gyllenhaal) are hired to tend sheep on Montana's Brokeback. In their remote campsite, the two men surprise themselves by becoming lovers. After the summer ends, they return to their separate lives. Both marry and have children, managing to ignore their feelings for one another until they meet again. At that point the consequences of both honesty and deception become apparent, showing that in real life there often is no "right" answer to the question of whether or not to reveal one's true identity.

You've Got Mail shows how identity management operates in mediated communication. Joe Fox (Tom Hanks) and Kathleen Kelly (Meg Ryan) are thirty-something New Yorkers who detest each other—at least in person. Face-to-face, Kathleen despises Joe because his discount bookstore chain threatens to bankrupt Kathleen's family-owned bookshop. She also hates Joe's arrogant, self-absorbed style of communicating. But in cyberspace, Joe seems like a different person. Unknown to both Joe and Kathleen, they have been communicating anonymously for months after meeting in an online chat room, using the names "NY152" and "Shopgirl." The e-mail messages Joe sends Kathleen are tender and self-disclosing. She falls for NY152 without knowing that the same man she can't stand in person writes the enchanting messages. For students of communication, this romance demonstrates that each of us has many identities and that the way we present ourselves can shape the fate of our relationships.

Shark Tale (2004, Rated PG)

Brokeback Mountain (2005, Rated R)

You've Got Mail (1999, Rated PG)

For more resources about identity management in film and television, see *Now Playing* at the *Understanding Human Communication* website at www.oup.com/us/uhc10.

self-monitors' ability to act means that it is difficult to tell how they are really feeling. In fact, because high self-monitors change roles often, they may have a hard time knowing *themselves* how they really feel.

People who score low on the self-monitoring scale live life quite differently from their more self-conscious counterparts. They have a simpler, more focused idea of who they are and who they want to be. Low self-monitors are likely to have a narrower repertoire of behaviors, so that they can be expected to act in more or less the same way regardless of the situation. This means that low self-monitors are easy to read. "What you see is what you get" might be their motto. Although this lack of flexibility may make their social interaction less smooth in many situations, low self-monitors can be counted on to be straightforward communicators.

By now it should be clear that neither extremely high nor low self-monitoring is the ideal. There are some situations when paying attention to yourself and adapting your behavior can be useful, but there are other situations when reacting without considering the effect on others is a better approach. This need for a range of behaviors demonstrates again the notion of communicative competence outlined in Chapter 1: Flexibility is the key to successful relationships.

Why Manage Identities?

Why bother trying to shape others' opinions? Sometimes we create and maintain a front to follow social rules. As children we learn to act polite, even when bored. Likewise, part of growing up consists of developing a set of manners for various occasions: meeting strangers, attending school, going to religious services, and so on. Young children who haven't learned all the do's and don'ts of polite society often embarrass their parents by behaving inappropriately ("Mommy, why is that man so fat?"), but by the time they enter school, behavior that might have been excusable or even amusing just isn't acceptable. Good manners are often aimed at making others more comfortable. For example, able-bodied people often mask their discomfort upon encountering someone who is disabled by acting nonchalant or stressing similarities between themselves and the disabled person.[77]

Social rules govern our behavior in a variety of settings. It would be impossible to keep a job, for example, without meeting certain expectations. Salespeople are obliged to treat customers with courtesy. Employees need to appear reasonably respectful when talking to the boss. Some forms of clothing would be considered outrageous at work. By agreeing to take on a job, you are signing an unwritten contract that you will present a certain face at work, whether or not that face reflects the way you might be feeling at a particular moment.

Even when social roles don't dictate the proper way to behave, we often manage identities for a second reason: to accomplish personal goals. You might, for example, dress up for a visit to traffic court in the hope that your front (responsible citizen) will convince the judge to treat you sympathetically. You might act sociable to your neighbors so they will agree to your request that they keep their dog off your lawn. We also try to create a desired impression to achieve one or more of the social needs described in Chapter 1: affection, inclusion, control, and so on. For instance, you might act more friendly and lively than you feel upon meeting a new person, so that you will appear likable. You could sigh and roll your eyes when arguing politics with a classmate to gain an advantage in an argument. You might smile and preen to show the attractive stranger at a party that you would like to get better acquainted. In situations like these you aren't being deceptive as much as putting "your best foot forward."

All these examples show that it is difficult—even impossible—*not* to create impressions. After all, you have to send *some* sort of message. If you don't act friendly when meeting a stranger, you have to act aloof, indifferent, hostile, or in some other manner. If you don't act businesslike, you have to behave in an alternative way: casual, goofy, or whatever. Often the question isn't whether or not to present a face to others; the question is only which face to present.

How Do We Manage Identities?

How do we create a public face? In an age when technology provides many options for communicating, the answer depends in part on the communication channel chosen.

Face-to-Face Impression Management In face-to-face interaction, communicators can manage their front in three ways: manner, appearance, and setting.[78] *Manner* consists of a communicator's words and nonverbal actions. Physicians, for example, display a wide variety of manners as they conduct physical examinations. Some are friendly and conversational, whereas others adopt a brusque and impersonal approach. Still others are polite but businesslike. Much of a communicator's manner comes from what he or she says. A doctor who remembers details about your interests and hobbies is quite different from one who sticks to clinical questions. Along with the content of

CULTURAL IDIOM
a front:
a pretense

putting "your best foot forward":
making the best appearance possible

speech, nonverbal behaviors play a big role in creating impressions. A doctor who greets you with a friendly smile and a handshake comes across quite differently from one who gives nothing more than a curt nod. The same principle holds in personal relationships. Your manner plays a major role in shaping how others view you. Chapters 3 and 5 will describe in detail how your words and nonverbal behaviors create impressions. Because you *have* to speak and act, the question isn't whether or not your manner sends messages; rather, the question is whether or not these messages will be intentional.

Along with manner, a second dimension of identity management is *appearance*—the personal items people use to shape an image. Sometimes appearance is part of creating a professional image. A physician's white lab coat and a police officer's uniform both set the wearer apart as someone special. A tailored suit or a rumpled outfit create very different impressions in the business world. Off the job, clothing is just as important. We choose clothing that sends a message about ourselves, sometimes trendy and sometimes traditional. Some people dress in ways that accent their sexuality, whereas others hide it. Clothing can say "I'm an athlete," "I'm wealthy," or "I'm an environmentalist." Along with dress, other aspects of appearance play a strong role in impression management. Are you suntanned or pale? What is your hair style?

A third way to manage impressions is through the choice of *setting*—physical items we use to influence how others view us. Consider the artifacts that people use to decorate the space where they live. For example, the posters and other items a college student uses to decorate her dorm room function as a kind of "who I am" statement.[79] In modern Western society the automobile is a major part of identity management. This explains why many people lust after cars that are far more expensive and powerful than they really need. A sporty convertible or fancy imported coupe doesn't just get drivers from one place to another: It also makes statements about the kind of people they are. The physical setting we choose and the way we arrange it are other important ways to manage impressions. What colors do you choose for the place you live? What artwork? What music do you play? Of course, we choose a setting that we enjoy, but in many cases we create an environment that will present the desired front to others. If you doubt this fact, just recall the last time you straightened up the house before important guests arrived. Backstage you might be comfortable with a messy place, but your public front—at least to some people—is quite different.

Identity Management in Computer Mediated Communication   At first glance, computer-mediated communication (CMC) seems to have limited potential for identity management. As you read in Chapter 1, text-based messages lack the "richness" of other channels. They don't convey the postures, gestures, or facial expressions that are an important part of face-to-face communication. They even lack the vocal information available in telephone messages. These limitations might seem to make it harder to create and manage an identity when communicating via computer.

Recently, though, communication scholars have begun to recognize that what is missing in CMC can actually be an *advantage* for communicators who want to manage the impressions they make.[80] E-mail authors can edit their

"I loved your E-mail, but I thought you'd be older."

messages until they create just the desired impression.[81] They can choose the desired level of clarity or ambiguity, seriousness or humor, logic or emotion. Unlike face-to-face communication, electronic correspondence allows a sender to say difficult things without forcing the receiver to respond immediately, and it permits the receiver to ignore a message rather than give an unpleasant response. Options like these show that CMC can serve as a tool for impression management at least as well as face-to-face communication.

CMC generally gives us more control over managing identities than we have in face-to-face communication. Asynchronous forms of CMC like e-mail, blogs, and web pages allow you to edit your messages until you convey the right impression. With e-mail (and, to a lesser degree, with instant messaging) you can compose difficult messages without forcing the receiver to respond immediately, and ignore others' messages rather than give an unpleasant response. Perhaps most important, with CMC you don't have to worry about stammering or blushing, apparel or appearance, or any other unseen factor that might detract from the impression you want to create.

CMC allows strangers to change their age, history, personality, appearance, and other matters that would be impossible to hide in person.[82] A quarter of teens have pretended to be a different person online, and a third confess to having given false information about themselves while e-mailing and instant messaging. A survey of one online dating site's participants found that 86 percent felt others misrepresented their physical appearance in their posted descriptions.[83] We'll talk about the ethics of such misrepresentations in the following section.

Like the one-to-one and small group channels of e-mail and instant messaging, "broadcasting" on the media is also a tool for managing one's identity. Blogs, personal web pages, and profiles on social networking websites like MySpace, FaceBook, and Friendster all provide opportunities for communicators to construct an identity.[84]

Identity Management and Honesty

After reading this far, you might think that identity management sounds like an academic label for manipulation or phoniness. If the perceived self is the "real" you, it might seem that any behavior that contradicts it would be dishonest.

There certainly are situations where identity management is dishonest. A manipulative date who pretends to be affectionate in order to gain sexual favors is clearly unethical and deceitful. So are job applicants who lie about academic records to get hired or salespeople who pretend to be dedicated to customer service when their real goal is to make a quick buck. But managing identities doesn't necessarily make you a liar. In fact, it is almost impossible to imagine how we could communicate effectively without making decisions about which front to present in one situation or another. It would be ludicrous for you to act the same way with strangers as you do with close friends, and nobody would show the same face to a two-year-old as to an adult.

Each of us has a repertoire of faces—a cast of characters—and part of being a competent communicator is choosing the best role for the situation. Consider a few examples:

- You have been communicating online for several weeks with someone you just met, and the relationship is starting to turn romantic. You have a physical trait that you haven't mentioned yet.

- You offer to teach a friend a new skill: playing the guitar, operating a computer program, or sharpening a tennis backhand. Your friend is making slow progress with the skill, and you find yourself growing impatient.

CULTURAL IDIOM
to make a quick buck:
to earn money with little effort

- At a party with a companion, you meet someone you find very attractive, and you are pretty sure that the feeling is mutual. You feel an obligation to spend most of your time with the person with whom you came, but the opportunity here is very appealing.

- At work you face a belligerent customer. You don't believe that anyone has the right to treat you this way.

- A friend or family member makes a joke about your appearance that hurts your feelings. You aren't sure whether to make an issue of the remark or pretend that it doesn't bother you.

In each of these situations—and in countless others every day—you have a choice about how to act. It is an oversimplification to say that there is only one honest way to behave in each circumstance and that every other response would be insincere and dishonest. Instead, impression management involves deciding which face—which part of yourself—to reveal. For example, when teaching a new skill you can choose to display the patient instead of the impatient side of yourself. In the same way, at work you have the option of acting hostile or nondefensive in difficult situations. With strangers, friends, or family you can choose whether or not to disclose your feelings. Which face to show to others is an important decision, but in any case you are sharing a real part of yourself. You may not be revealing *everything*—but, as you will learn in Chapter 6, complete self-disclosure is rarely appropriate.

ETHICAL CHALLENGE

● **Honesty and Multiple Identities**

Your text argues that presenting different identities to the world isn't inherently dishonest. Nonetheless, there are certainly cases when it is deceitful to construct an identity that doesn't match your private self.

You can explore the ethics of multiple identities by identifying two situations from your life:

1. A time when you presented a public identity that didn't match your private self in a manner that wasn't unethical.

2. A situation (real or hypothetical) in which you have presented or could present a dishonest identity.

Based on the situations you and your classmates present, develop a code of ethics that identifies the boundary between ethical and unethical identity management.

Summary

Perceptions of others are always selective and are often distorted. The chapter began by describing how personal narratives shape our perceptions. It then outlined several perceptual errors that can affect the way we view and communicate with others. Along with universal psychological influences, cultural factors affect perceptions. Increased empathy is a valuable tool for increasing understanding of others and hence communicating more effectively with them. Perception checking is one tool for increasing the accuracy of perceptions and for increasing empathy.

Perceptions of one's self are just as subjective as perceptions of others, and they influence communication at least as much. Although individuals are born with some innate personality characteristics, the self-concept is shaped dramatically by communication with others, as well as by cultural factors. Once established, the self-concept can lead us to create self-fulfilling prophecies that determine how we behave and how others respond to us.

Impression management consists of strategic communication designed to influence others' perceptions of an individual. Impression management operates when we seek, consciously or unconsciously, to present one or more public faces to others. These faces may be different from the private, spontaneous behavior that occurs outside of others' presence. Identity management is usually collaborative: Communication goes most smoothly when we communicate in ways that support others' faces, and they support ours. Some communicators are high self-monitors who are intensely conscious of their own behavior, whereas others are low self-monitors who are less aware of how their words and actions affect others.

Identity management occurs for two reasons. In many cases it aims at following social rules and conventions. In other cases it aims at achieving a variety of content and relational goals. In either case, communicators engage in creating impressions by managing their manner, appearance, and the settings in which they interact with others. Although identity management might seem manipulative, it can be an authentic form of communication. Because each person has a variety of faces that he or she can present, choosing which one to present need not be dishonest.

Key Terms

empathy 50	presenting self 54
ethnocentrism 50	reflected appraisal 34
face 54	selection 41
facework 54	self-concept 32
identity	self-esteem 33
management 54	self-fulfilling
interpretation 42	prophecy 38
narratives 43	self-serving bias 45
organization 41	significant others 34
perceived self 54	stereotyping 44
perception checking 53	sympathy 51
personality 38	

Activities

1. **Exploring Narratives** Think about a situation where relational harmony is due to you and the other people involved sharing the same narrative. Then think about another situation where you and the other person use different narratives to describe the same situation. What are the consequences of having different narratives in this situation?

2. **Experiencing Another Culture** Spend at least an hour in a culture that is unfamiliar to you and where you are a minority. Visit an area where another cultural, age, or ethnic group is the majority. Attend a meeting or patronize an establishment where you are in the minority. Observe how communication practices differ from those of your own culture. Based on

your experience, discuss what you can do to facilitate communication with people from other cultural backgrounds whom you may encounter in your everyday life. (As you develop a list of ideas, realize that what you might consider helpful behavior could make communicators from different cultures even more uncomfortable.)

3. **Empathy Exercise** Choose a disagreement you presently have with another person or group. The disagreement might be a personal one—such as an argument about how to settle a financial problem or who is to blame for a present state of affairs—or it might be a dispute over a contemporary public issue, such as the right of women to obtain abortions on demand or the value of capital punishment.

   1. In three hundred words or so, describe your side of the issue. State why you believe as you do, just as if you were presenting your position to an important jury.

   2. Now take three hundred words or so to describe in the first-person singular the other person's perspective on the same issue. For instance, if you are a religious person, write this section as if you were an atheist: For a short while get in touch with how the other person feels and thinks.

   3. Now show the description you wrote to your "opponent," the person whose beliefs are different from yours. Have that person read your account and correct any statements that don't reflect his or her position accurately. Remember: You're doing this so that you can more clearly understand how the issue looks to the other person.

   4. Make any necessary corrections in the account you wrote, and again show it to your partner. When your partner agrees that you understand his or her position, have your partner sign your paper to indicate this.

   5. Now record your conclusions to this experiment. Has this perceptual shift made any difference in how you view the issue or how you feel about your partner?

4. **Perception-Checking Practice** Practice your perception-checking ability by developing three-part verifications for the following situations:

   1. You made what you thought was an excellent suggestion to an instructor. The instructor looked uninterested but said she would check on the matter right away. Three weeks have passed, and nothing has changed.

   2. A neighbor and good friend has not responded to your "Good morning" for three days in a row. This person is usually friendly.

   3. You haven't received the usual weekly phone call from the folks back home in over a month. The last time you spoke, you had an argument about where to spend the holidays.

   4. An old friend with whom you have shared the problems of your love life for years has recently changed when around you: The formerly casual hugs and kisses have become longer and stronger, and the occasions where you "accidentally" brush up against one another have become more frequent.

5. **Identifying Your Identities** Keep a one-day log listing the identities you create in different situations: at school, at work, and with strangers, various family members, and different friends. For each identity,

1. Describe the persona you are trying to project (e.g., "responsible son or daughter," "laid-back friend," "attentive student").

2. Explain how you communicate to promote this identity. What kinds of things do you say (or not say)? How do you act?

For Further Exploration

For more resources about the self and perception, see the *Understanding Human Communication* website at www.oup.com/us/uhc10. There you will find a variety of resources: a list of books and articles, links to descriptions of feature films and television shows at the *Now Playing* website, study aids, and a self-test to check your understanding of the material in this chapter.

CHAPTER HIGHLIGHTS

Language has several important characteristics:

- It is symbolic.
- Meanings reside in the minds of people, not in words themselves.
- It is governed by several types of rules, and understanding those rules helps us understand one another.

Beyond simply expressing ideas, language can be very powerful:

- It can shape our attitudes toward things and toward one another.
- It can reflect the way we feel about things and people.

Some kinds of language can create problems by unnecessarily:

- Disrupting relationships
- Confusing others
- Avoiding important information

Gender plays an important role in the way language operates:

- The content of male and female speech varies somewhat.
- Men and women often have different reasons for communicating.
- Male and female conversational style varies in some interesting ways.
- Gender isn't always the most important factor in shaping language use.

Cultural factors can shape the way we see and understand language:

- Different cultures have different notions of what language styles are and aren't appropriate.
- The language we speak can shape the way we view the world.

CHAPTER 3

Language

After studying the material in this chapter . . .

You should understand:

1. The symbolic, person-centered nature of language.
2. Phonological, semantic, syntactic, and pragmatic rules that govern language.
3. The ways in which language shapes and reflects attitudes.
4. The types of troublesome language and the skills to deal with each.
5. The gender and nongender factors that characterize the speech of men and women.
6. The verbal styles that distinguish various cultures, and the effect that language can have on worldview.

You should be able to:

1. Discuss how you and others use syntactic, semantic, phonological, and pragmatic rules and how their use affects a message's comprehension.
2. Identify at least two ways in which language has shaped your attitudes.
3. Identify at least two ways in which language reflects your attitudes.
4. Recognize and suggest alternatives for equivocal language, slang and jargon, relative terms, and overly abstract language.
5. Identify and suggest alternatives for fact-inference and fact-opinion confusion and for emotive statements.
6. Suggest appropriate alternatives for unnecessary or misleading euphemisms and equivocal statements.
7. Identify the degree to which your speech reflects gender stereotypes, and then reflect on the effect your cultural speech patterns have on others.

At one time or another, every one of us has suffered the limits and traps of language. Even though we are using familiar words, it's clear that we often don't use them in ways that allow us to communicate smoothly with one another.

In the following pages we will explore the nature of linguistic communication. By the time you have finished reading this chapter, you will better appreciate the complexity of language, its power to shape our perception of people and events, and its potential for incomplete and inaccurate communication. Perhaps more importantly, you will be better equipped to use the tool of language more skillfully to improve your everyday interaction.

The Nature of Language

Humans speak about ten thousand dialects.[1] Although most of these sound different from one another, all possess the same characteristics of **language:** a collection of symbols governed by rules and used to convey messages between individuals. A closer look at this definition can explain how language operates and suggest how we can use it more effectively.

Language Is Symbolic

There's nothing natural about calling your loyal four-footed companion a "dog" or the object you're reading right now a "book." These words, like virtually all language, are **symbols**—arbitrary constructions that represent a communicator's thoughts. Not all linguistic symbols are spoken or written words. Sign language, as "spoken" by most deaf people, is symbolic in nature and not the pantomime it might seem. There are literally hundreds of different sign languages spoken around the world that represent

"What part of oil lamp next to double squiggle over ox don't you understand?"

the same ideas differently.[2] These distinct languages include American Sign Language, British Sign Language, French Sign Language, Danish Sign Language, Chinese Sign Language—even Australian Aboriginal and Mayan sign languages.

Symbols are more than just labels: They are the way we experience the world. You can prove this by trying a simple experiment.[3] Work up some saliva in your mouth, and then spit it into a glass. Take a good look, and then drink it up. Most people find this process mildly disgusting. But ask yourself why this is so. After all, we swallow our own saliva all the time. The answer arises out of the symbolic labels we use. After the saliva is in the glass, we call it *spit* and think of it in a different way. In other words, our reaction is to the *name*, not the thing.

The naming process operates in virtually every situation. How you react to a stranger will depend on the symbols you use to categorize him or her: gay (or straight), religious (or not), attractive (or unattractive), and so on.

Meanings Are in People, Not Words

Ask a dozen people what the same symbol means, and you are likely to get twelve different answers. Does an American flag bring up associations of patriots giving their lives for their country? Fourth of July parades? Cultural imperialism? How about a cross: What does it represent? The message of Jesus Christ? Fire-lit rallies of Ku Klux Klansmen? Your childhood Sunday school? The necklace your sister always wears?

As with physical symbols, the place to look for meaning in language isn't in the words themselves, but rather in the way people make sense of them. One unfortunate example of this fact occurred in Washington, DC, when the newly appointed city ombudsman used the word "niggardly" to describe an approach to budgeting.[4] Some African-American critics accused him of uttering an unforgivable racial slur. His defenders pointed out that the word, which means "miserly," is derived from Scandinavian languages and that it has no link to the racial slur it resembles. Even though the criticisms eventually died away, they illustrate that, correct or not, the meanings people associate with words have far more significance than do their dictionary definitions.

Linguistic theorists C. K. Ogden and I. A. Richards illustrated the fact that meanings are social constructions in their well-known "triangle of meaning" (Figure 3-1).[5] This model shows that there is only an indirect relationship—indicated by a broken line—between a word and the thing it claims to represent. Some of these "things" or referents do not exist in the physical world. For instance, some referents are mythical (such as unicorns), some are no longer tangible (such as Elvis, if he really is dead), and others are abstract ideas (such as "love").

Problems arise when people mistakenly assume that others use words in the same way they do. It's possible to have an argument about *feminism* without ever realizing that you and the other person are using the word to represent entirely different things. The same goes for *environmentalism*, *Republicans*, *rock music*, and thousands upon thousands of other symbols. Words don't mean; people do—and often in widely different ways.

Despite the potential for linguistic problems, the situation isn't hopeless. We do, after all, communicate with one another reasonably well most of the time. And with enough effort, we

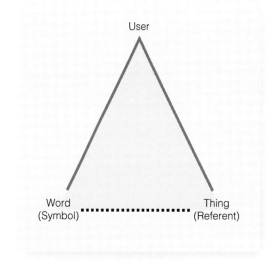

FIGURE 3-1　Ogden and Richards's Triangle of Meaning

UNDERSTANDING COMMUNICATION TECHNOLOGY
Translation on the Web

Can technology solve the ages-old problem of allowing us to understand people who speak different languages? Several sites on the World Wide Web offer automatic computerized translations. One such program is available free through AltaVista at http://world.altavista.com/.

How effective are programs like AltaVista's? The standard way to test the accuracy of a translator is to convert a message from one language to another, and then back. This approach demonstrates that computerized translations are useful, but far from perfect.

AltaVista's software works well enough for most simple messages. For example, the request "Please send me information on travel in Latin America." came through almost perfectly when first translated into Spanish and then back to English.

A translation of the announcement "My flight from Miami arrives at 9:00 P.M." changed prepositions, but it was understandable when it came back as "My flight of Miami arrives 9:00 P.M."

Translation software begins to show its limitations when literal conversions fail to capture the colloquial meaning of a word. For example, the message "This is a tricky job" came back from AltaVista after an Italian translation as "This is a deceptive job." It's easy to imagine how this sort of error could lead to ill feelings.

Idioms are especially prone to bungled translations. For example, the English expression "That's easier said than done" was translated in an English-Spanish-English conversion into the confusing statement "That one is the this easiest one that done." An English-French-English translation of "I'm down in the dumps" came back as "I am feeling downwards in emptyings."

Computerized translations aren't advised for communicators who want to build and maintain personal relationships. A simple example shows why: The flattering confession "I would like to get to know you better" was transformed into the confusing statement "It wanted to familiarize to me with him better"—not the kind of message that is likely to win friends and influence people.

Despite their shortcomings, computerized translation programs can provide at least a sense of what is being expressed in an unfamiliar language. At the same time, their flaws demonstrate that understanding semantic and pragmatic rules is a uniquely human ability—at least for now.

can clear up most of the misunderstandings that do occur. The key to more accurate use of language is to avoid assuming that others interpret words the same way we do. In truth, successful communication occurs when we *negotiate* the meaning of a statement.[6] As one French proverb puts it: The spoken word belongs half to the one who speaks it and half to the one who hears.

Language Is Rule Governed

Languages contain several types of rules. **Phonological rules** govern how words sound when pronounced. For instance, the words *champagne, double,* and *occasion* are spelled identically in French and English, but all are pronounced differently. Nonnative speakers learning English are plagued by inconsistent phonological rules, as a few examples illustrate:

He could lead if he would get the lead out.
A farm can produce produce.
The dump was so full it had to refuse refuse.
The present is a good time to present the present.
I did not object to the object.
The bandage was wound around the wound.
I shed a tear when I saw the tear in my clothes.

Phonological rules aren't the only ones that govern the way we use language to communicate. **Syntactic rules** govern the structure of language—the way symbols can be arranged. For example, correct English syntax requires that every word contain at least one vowel and prohibits sentences such as "Have you the cookies brought?" which is a perfectly acceptable word order in German. Although most of us aren't able to describe the syntactic rules that govern our language, it's easy to recognize their existence by noting how odd a statement that violates them appears.

Technology has spawned subversions of English with their own syntactic rules.[7] For example, users of instant messaging on the Internet have devised a streamlined version of English that speeds up typing in real-time communication (although it probably makes teachers of composition grind their teeth in anguish):

A: Hey

B: r u at home?

A: yup yup

B: ok I'm getting offline now

A: no! why?

B: i need t study for finals u can call me tho bye

A: kbye

Semantic rules deal with the meaning of specific words. Semantic rules are what make it possible for us to agree that "bikes" are for riding and "books" are for reading; they also help us to know whom we will and won't encounter when we open doors marked "men" or "women." Without semantic rules, communication would be impossible, because each of us would use symbols in unique ways, unintelligible to one another.

Semantic misunderstandings occur when words can be interpreted in more than one way, as the following humorous notices prove:

The peacemaking meeting scheduled for today has been cancelled due to a conflict.

For those of you who have children and don't know it, we have a nursery downstairs.

The ladies of the Church have cast off clothing of every kind. They may be seen in the basement on Friday afternoon.

Sunday's sermon topic will be "What Is Hell?" Come early and listen to our choir practice.

Read about the Fighting Whites basketball team at http://en-wikipedia.org/wiki/Fighting_Whites. Do you agree with the rationale behind the team's name? How does it compare with athletic teams named after other ethnic groups (e.g., Indians)? Are there times when it is acceptable to use ethnic labels in a humorous way? What pragmatic rules govern the use of these terms?

CRITICAL THINKING PROBE

● **When Is Language Offensive?**

Pragmatic rules govern how people use language in everyday interaction, which communication theorists have characterized as a series of *speech acts*.[8] Consider the example of a male boss saying "You look very pretty today" to a female employee. It's easy to imagine how the subordinate might be offended by a comment that her boss considered an innocent remark. Scholars of language have pointed out several levels at which the rules each person uses can differ. You can understand these levels by imagining how they would operate in our example:

Each person's self-concept
Boss: Views himself as a nice guy.
Subordinate: Determined to succeed on her own merits, and not her appearance.

The episode in which the comment occurs
Boss: Casual remark at the start of the workday.
Employee: A possible come-on?

Perceived relationship
Boss: Views employees like members of the family.
Employee: Depends on boss's goodwill for advancement.

Cultural background
Boss: Member of generation in which comments about appearance were common.
Employee: Member of generation sensitive to sexual harassment.

As this example shows, pragmatic rules don't involve semantic issues, since the words themselves are usually understood well by almost everybody. Instead, they involve how those words are understood and used. For another example of how pragmatic rules can shape understanding and interaction, see the Critical Thinking Probe on page 71.

The Power of Language

On the most obvious level, language allows us to satisfy basic functions such as describing ideas, making requests, and solving problems. But beyond these functions, the way we use language also influences others and reflects our attitudes in more subtle ways, which we will examine now.

"Look, I'd rather be free, too, but at least we're not in a zoo anymore."

Language Shapes Attitudes

The power of language to shape ideas has been recognized throughout history. The first chapters of the Bible report that Adam's dominion over animals was demonstrated by his being given the power to give them names.[9] As we will now see, our speech—sometimes consciously and sometimes not—shapes others' values, attitudes, and beliefs in a variety of ways.

Naming   "What's in a name?" Juliet asked rhetorically. If Romeo had been a social scientist, he would have answered, "A great deal." Research has demonstrated that names are more than just a simple means of identification: They shape the way others think of us, the way we view ourselves, and the way we act.

At the most fundamental level, some research suggests that even the phonetic sound of a person's name affects the way we regard him or her, at least when we don't have other information available. One study revealed that reasonably accurate predictions about who will win an election can be made on the basis of some phonetic features of the candidates' surnames.[10] Names that were simple, easily pronounced, and rhythmic were judged more favorably than ones that lack these qualities. For example, in one series of local elections, the winning candidates had names that resonated with voters: Sanders beat Pekelis, Rielly defeated Dellwo, Grady outpolled Schumacher, Combs trounced Bernsdorf, and Golden prevailed over Nuffer. Names don't guarantee victory, but in seventy-eight elections, forty-eight outcomes supported the value of having an appealing name.

Names are one way to shape and reinforce a child's personal identity. Naming a baby after a family member (e.g., "Junior" or "Trey") can create a connection between the youngster and his or her namesake. Name choice can also be a powerful way to make a statement about cultural identity. For example, in recent decades a large percentage of names given to African-American babies have been distinctively black.[11] In California, over 40 percent of black girls born recently have names that not a single white baby born in the entire state was given. Researchers suggest that distinctive names like these are a symbol of solidarity with the African-American community. Conversely, choosing a less distinctive name can be a way of integrating the baby into the majority culture. Whether common or unusual, the impact of names recedes after communicators become more familiar with one another.[12]

Choosing a newborn's name can be especially challenging for people from non-dominant cultures with different languages. One writer from India describes the problem he and his wife faced when considering names for their first child:

> How will the child's foreign name sound to American ears? (That test ruled out Shiva, my family deity; a Jewish friend put her foot down.) Will it provoke bullies to beat him up on the school playground? (That was the end of Karan, the name of a warrior from the Mahabharata, the Hindu epic. A boy called "Karen" wouldn't stand a chance.) Will it be as euphonic in New York as it is in New Delhi? (That was how Sameer failed to get off the ground. "Like a bagel with a schmear!" said one ruthless well-wisher.)[13]

First names aren't the only linguistic elements that may shape attitudes about men and women. As the reading on page 74 suggests, the choice of what last name to use after marriage can influence others' perceptions.

Credibility   Scholarly speaking is a good example of how speech style influences perception. We refer to what has been called the Dr. Fox hypothesis.[14] "An apparently legitimate speaker who utters an unintelligible message will be judged competent by an audience in the speaker's area of apparent expertise." The Dr. Fox hypothesis got its name from one Dr. Myron L. Fox, who delivered a talk followed by a half-hour discussion on "Mathematical Game Theory as Applied to Physical Education." The audience included psychiatrists, psychologists, social workers, and educators. Questionnaires collected after the session revealed that these educated listeners found the lecture clear and stimulating.

Despite his warm reception by this learned audience, Fox was a complete fraud. He was a professional actor whom researchers had coached to deliver a lecture of double-talk—a patchwork of information from a *Scientific American* article mixed with jokes, non sequiturs, contradictory statements, and meaningless references to unrelated topics. When wrapped in a linguistic package of high-level professional jargon, however, the meaningless gobbledygook was judged as important information. In other

INVITATION TO INSIGHT

In the Name of Love

It used to be a non-issue. When Jane Doe married Joe Snow, she became Jane Snow. But as gender roles change, more couples are breaking with tradition.

These days, a married woman might remain Jane Doe or become Jane Doe Snow, or Jane Doe-Snow—or her husband might become Joe Doe. Some couples are choosing to merge their last names, becoming Jane and Joe Snowdoe.

"There's been all kinds of engineering with names," says Rae Moses, a linguistics professor at Northwestern University. Moses surveyed an Illinois grade school with 302 students and found that 32% of them—most of whose mothers were working professionals—had nontraditional last names.

As more options become acceptable, many couples are asking themselves: What's in a name?

There's no shortage of answers. To some, the traditional method is a sexist vestige of the days when a woman literally became her husband's property. To others, the tradition has long since shed that stigma and has become a romantic symbol of the bond between two people. To still others, it's a convenient way to dump an unwieldy name. At least 90% of Americans still follow tradition, says Laurie Scheuble, a sociologist at Doane College in Nebraska. But, she says, as more women establish careers and marry later in life, many are choosing to keep their names.

"I don't think it's ever going to be the norm, but I think we're going to see more of it in the future," says Scheuble. She adds,

people with more education and higher incomes are more likely to be tolerant of a woman keeping her name, as are people who grew up in large cities. Political and religious leanings also seemed to affect attitudes.

When Jeff Nicholson of Champaign, Ill., married Dawn Owens, he became Nicholson-Owens; she became Owens-Nicholson. "I felt it would make me feel a lot closer to her," says Jeff, 24. "And it seemed fairest. Neither of us loses our heritage in the family tree." Dawn, 31, says her family wasn't thrilled when she broke the news. "My mom was really looking forward to saying 'Mr. and Mrs. Jeffrey Nicholson.'" So, apparently, was the Illinois Department of Motor Vehicles. "We had to fight them tooth and nail to get a hyphen on our driver's licenses," Dawn says. "They said their software wouldn't take it."

Nancy Herman of Minneapolis and her husband, Don Perlmutter, came up with yet another variation: They merged their names, becoming the Perlmans.

Several other countries do have different naming methods. In some Scandinavian and Latin American countries, married women often keep their names. In Japan, if a woman with no siblings marries into a family that has several sons, her husband will sometimes take her family name. "It's kind of a gift that the groom's family gives to the bride's family," Moses says.

Suzanne Schlosberg

words, Fox's audience reaction was based more on the credibility that arose from his use of impressive-sounding language than from the ideas he expressed.

The same principle seems to hold for academic writing.[15] A group of thirty-two management professors rated material according to its complexity rather than its content. When a message about consumer behavior was loaded with unnecessary words and long, complex sentences, the professors rated it highly. When the same message was translated into more readable English, with shorter words and clearer sentences, the professors judged the same research as less competent.

Status   In the classic musical *My Fair Lady*, Professor Henry Higgins transformed Eliza Doolittle from a lowly flower girl into a high-society woman by replacing her cockney accent with an upper-crust speaking style. Decades of research have demonstrated that the power of speech to influence status is a fact.[16] Several factors combine to create positive or negative impressions: accent, choice of words, speech rate, and even the apparent age of a speaker. In most cases, speakers of standard dialect are rated higher than nonstandard speakers in a variety of ways: They are viewed as more competent and more self-confident, and the content of their messages is rated more favorably. The unwillingness or inability of a communicator to use the standard dialect fluently can have serious consequences. For instance, speakers of Black English, a distinctive dialect with its own accent, grammar, syntax, and semantic rules, are rated as less intelligent, professional, capable, socially acceptable, and employable by speakers of standard English.[17]

Sexism and Racism   By now it should be clear that the power of language to shape attitudes goes beyond individual cases and influences how we perceive entire groups of people. For example, Casey Miller and Kate Swift argue that incorrect use of the pronoun *he* to refer to both men and women can have damaging results.

> On the television screen, a teacher of first-graders who has just won a national award is describing her way of teaching. "You take each child where you find him," she says. "You watch to see what he's interested in, and then you build on his interests."
> A five-year-old looking at the program asks her mother, "Do only boys go to that school?"
> "No," her mother begins, "she's talking about girls too, but—"
> But what? The teacher being interviewed on television is speaking correct English. What can the mother tell her daughter about why a child, in any generalization, is always he rather than she? How does a five-year-old comprehend the generic personal pronoun?[18]

It's usually easy to use nonsexist language. For example, the term *mankind* may be replaced by *humanity, human beings, human race,* or *people; man-made* may be replaced by *artificial, manufactured,* and *synthetic; manpower* may be replaced by *human power, workers,* and *workforce;* and *manhood* may be replaced by *adulthood.*

The use of labels for racist purposes has a long and ugly past. Names have been used throughout history to stigmatize groups that other groups have disapproved of.[19] By using derogatory terms to label some people, the out-group is set apart and pictured in an unfavorable light. Diane Mader provides several examples of this:

> We can see the process of stigmatization in Nazi Germany when Jewish people became vermin, in the United States when African Americans became "niggers" and chattel, in the military when the Vietnam-era enemy became "gooks."[20]

The power of racist language to shape attitudes is difficult to avoid, even when it is obviously offensive. In one study, experimental subjects who heard a derogatory label used against a member of a minority group expressed annoyance at this sort of slur, but despite their disapproval, the negative emotional terms did have an impact.[21] Not only did the unwitting subjects rate the minority individual's competence lower when that person performed poorly, but also they found fault with others who associated socially with the minority person—even members of the subject's own ethnic group.

One of the most treasured civil liberties is freedom of speech. At the same time, most people would agree that some forms of racist and sexist speech are hateful and demeaning to their targets. As you have read in these pages, language shapes the attitudes of those who hear it.

How do you reconcile the principle of free speech and the need to minimize hateful and discriminatory messages? Do you think laws and policies can and should be made that limit certain types of communication? If so, how should those limits be drafted to protect civil liberties? If not, can you justify the necessary protection of even sexist and racist language?

ETHICAL CHALLENGE

● **Sexist and Racist Language**

Language Reflects Attitudes

Besides shaping the way we view ourselves and others, language reflects our attitudes. Feelings of control, attraction, commitment, responsibility—all these and more are reflected in the way we use language.

Power Communication researchers have identified a number of language patterns that add to, or detract from, a speaker's ability to influence others, as well as reflecting how a speaker feels about his or her degree of control over a situation.[22] Table 3-1 summarizes some of these findings by listing several types of "powerless" language.

You can see the difference between powerful language and powerless language by comparing the following statements:

> "Excuse me, sir, I hate to say this, but I . . . uh . . . I guess I won't be able to turn in the assignment on time. I had a personal emergency and . . . well . . . it was just impossible to finish it by today. I'll have it in your mailbox on Monday, okay?"
>
> "I won't be able to turn in the assignment on time. I had a personal emergency, and it was impossible to finish it by today. I'll have it in your mailbox on Monday."

Although the powerless speech described in Table 3-1 can often lead to unsatisfying results, don't assume that the best goal is always to sound as powerful as you can. Along with gaining compliance, another conversational goal is often building a supportive, friendly relationship, and sharing power with the other person can help you in this regard. For this reason, many everyday statements will contain a mixture of powerful speech and powerless speech. Our student-teacher example illustrates how this combination of powerless mannerisms and powerful mannerisms can help the student get what she wants while staying on good terms with the professor:

> "Excuse me, Professor Rodman. I want you to know that I won't be able to turn in the assignment on time. I had a personal emergency, and it was impossible to finish it by today. I'll definitely have it in your mailbox on Monday."

Whether or not the professor finds the excuse acceptable, it's clear that this last statement combines the best features of powerful speech and powerless speech: a combination of self-assurance and goodwill.

Simply counting the number of powerful or powerless statements won't always reveal who has the most control in a relationship. Social rules often mask the real distribution of power. Sociolinguist Deborah Tannen describes how politeness can be a face-saving way of delivering an order:

> I hear myself giving instructions to my assistants without actually issuing orders: "Maybe it would be a good idea to . . .;" "It would be great if you could . . ." all the while knowing that I expect them to do what I've asked right away . . . This rarely creates problems, though, because the people who work for me know that there is only one reason I mention tasks—because I want them done. I *like* giving instructions in this way; it appeals to my sense of what it means to be a good person . . . taking others' feelings into account.[23]

As this quote suggests, high-status speakers often realize that politeness is an effective way to get their needs met while protecting the face of the less powerful person. The importance of achieving both content goals and relational goals helps explain why a mixture of powerful speech and polite speech is usually most effective.[24] Of course, if the other person misinterprets politeness for weakness, it may be necessary to shift to a more powerful speaking style.

Powerful speech that gets the desired results in mainstream North American and European culture doesn't succeed everywhere with everyone.[25] In Japan, saving face for others is an important goal, so communicators there tend to speak in ambiguous terms and use hedge words and qualifiers. In most Japanese sentences the verb comes at the end of the sentence so the "action" part of the statement can be postponed. Traditional Mexican culture, with its strong emphasis on cooperation, makes a priority of using language to create harmony in interpersonal relationships, rather than taking a firm or oppositional stance, in order to make others feel more at ease. Korean culture represents yet another group of people that prefers "indirect" (for example, "perhaps," "could be") to "direct" speech.

TABLE 3-1 Powerless Language

Type of Usage	Example
Hedges	"I'm kinda disappointed . . ." "I think we should . . ." "I guess I'd like to . . ."
Hesitations	"Uh, can I have a minute of your time?" "Well, we could try this idea . . ." "I wish you would—er—try to be on time."
Intensifiers	"So that's how I feel . . ." "I'm not very hungry."
Polite forms	"Excuse me, sir . . ."
Tag questions	"It's about time we got started, isn't it?" "Don't you think we should give it another try?"
Disclaimers	"I probably shouldn't say this, but . . ." "I'm not really sure, but . . ."

Affiliation Power isn't the only way language reflects the status of relationships. Language can also be a way of building and demonstrating solidarity with others. An impressive body of research has demonstrated that communicators who want to show affiliation with one another adapt their speech in a variety of ways, including their choice of vocabulary, rate of talking, number and placement of pauses, and level of politeness.[26] On an individual level, close friends and lovers often develop special terms that serve as a way of signifying their relationship.[27] Using the same vocabulary sets these people apart from others, reminding themselves and the rest of the world of their relationship. The same process works among members of larger groups, ranging from street gangs to military personnel. Communication researchers call this linguistic accommodation **convergence.**

Communicators can experience convergence in cyberspace as well as in face-to-face interactions. Members of online communities often develop a shared language and conversational style, and their affiliation with each other can be seen in increased uses of the pronoun "we."[28] On a larger scale, IM and e-mail users create and use shortcuts that mark them as Internet-savvy. If you know what ROTF, IMHO, and JK mean, you're probably part of that group. (For the uninitiated, those acronyms mean "Rolling on the floor laughing," "In my humble opinion," and "Just kidding.") Interestingly, instant-messagers may find that their cyberlanguage creeps into everyday conversations.[29] (Have you ever said "LOL" instead of the words "laughing out loud"—or instead of actually laughing out loud?)

When two or more people feel equally positive about one another, their linguistic convergence will be mutual. But when communicators want or need the approval of others they often adapt their speech to suit the others' style, trying to say the "right thing" or speak in a way that will help them fit in. We see this process when immigrants who want to gain the rewards of material success in a new culture strive to master the prevalent language. Likewise, employees who seek advancement tend to speak more like their superiors: supervisors adopt the speech style of managers, and managers converge toward their bosses.

CULTURAL IDIOM

saving face:
protecting one's dignity

MEDIA ROOM
Linguistic Convergence and Divergence

Using similar terms and speech patterns can be a tool for building solidarity. Conversely, different language styles can both create and reflect social differences. The films described illustrate how challenging and fascinating the unspoken rules of convergence and divergence can be.

In *The Pacifier,* Shane Wolfe (Vin Diesel) is a brash undercover agent and ex-Navy SEAL who cares for the five children of a scientist whose death he feels responsible for causing. Wolfe has no experience with children, and he relies on his military style to communicate with his young charges. He barks out orders, calls the family's car an "assault vehicle," and renames the children "Red One, Red Two, Red Three, Red Four and Red Baby" since he can't remember their actual names. In the end, the children and Wolfe learn to adapt to each other's linguistic norms, offering an entertaining example of how linguistic convergence can help build relationships.

In *Mean Girls,* we meet Cady Heron (Lindsay Lohan), just back to the United States from the African bush country where she was raised by her zoologist parents. For Cady, part of fitting in at North Shore High is to learn and use the vocabulary of the in-group "Plastics." In an early conversation with these popular girls, their leader Regina (Rachel McAdams) exclaims to Cady, "Shut Up!" Unfamiliar with the slang use of this term, Cady replies, "I didn't say anything." Soon Cady speaks Plastic fluently, tossing about words like "fetch" (cool), "word vomit" (babbling), and the self-explanatory "fugly."

In an interesting example of linguistic convergence, the more Cady "talks the talk" of being a Plastic, the more her values and behaviors become like theirs. By movie's end, she makes some important decisions about herself and her friends—including the decision not to talk or act like a "mean girl."

The N Word refers to what is possibly the most inflammatory word in American culture—so much so that the letter "N" is substituted for the actual word in most public discussions. But as this documentary shows, the "N word" has many and varied meanings, ranging from a degrading slur to a term of endearment. A host of scholars and celebrities (including Chris Rock, Whoopi Goldberg, George Carlin, Ice Cube, and Quincy Jones) discuss and debate when, where, how, by whom, and even whether the "N word" should be used. The film offers a vivid illustration of how complicated the rules of language use can be, and how the same term can be either a form of convergence or divergence.

Many television medical dramatic series (e.g., *House, Grey's Anatomy, ER*) illustrate linguistic convergence and divergence. As in real life, medical professionals in these shows make influential linguistic choices about whether or not to explain conditions and treatments to patients in nonmedical language (convergence) or to use professional jargon that, while more succinct, exmphasizes their membership in a separate group.

The Pacifier (2005, Rated PG)

Mean Girls (2004, Rated PG-13)

The N Word (2004, Not Rated)

House (2004– , Rated TV-PG)

Grey's Anatomy (2005– , Rated TV-14)

ER (1994– , Rated TV-14)

For more resources about identity management in film and television, see *Now Playing* at the *Understanding Human Communication* website at www.oup.com/us/uhc10.

The principle of speech accommodation works in reverse, too. Communicators who want to set themselves apart from others adopt the strategy of **divergence,** speaking in a way that emphasizes their difference from others. For example, members of an ethnic group, even though fluent in the dominant language, might use their own dialect as a way of showing solidarity with one another—a sort of "us against them" strategy. Divergence also operates in other settings. A physician or attorney, for example, who wants to establish credibility with his or her client might speak formally and use professional jargon to create a sense of distance. The implicit message here is "I'm different (and more knowledgeable) than you."

Attraction and Interest   Social customs discourage us from expressing like or dislike in many situations. Only a clod would respond to the question "What do you think of the cake I baked for you?" by saying, "It's terrible." Bashful or cautious suitors might

CULTURAL IDIOM
a clod:
a dull or stupid person

not admit their attraction to a potential partner. Even when people are reluctant to speak candidly, the language they use can suggest their degree of interest and attraction toward a person, object, or idea. Morton Weiner and Albert Mehrabian outline a number of linguistic clues that reveal these attitudes.[30]

- **Demonstrative pronoun choice.** *These* people want our help (positive) versus *Those* people want our help (less positive).
- **Negation.** It's *good* (positive) versus It's *not bad* (less positive).
- **Sequential placement.** Dick and Jane (Dick is more important) versus Jane and Dick (Jane is more important). However, sequential placement isn't always significant. You may put "toilet bowl cleaner" at the top of your shopping list simply because it's closer to the market door than is champagne.

Responsibility   In addition to suggesting liking and importance, language can reveal the speaker's willingness to accept responsibility for a message.

- **"It" versus "I" statements.** *It's* not finished (less responsible) versus *I* didn't finish it (more responsible).
- **"You" versus "I" statements.** Sometimes *you* make me angry (less responsible) versus Sometimes *I* get angry when you do that (more responsible). "I" statements are more likely to generate positive reactions from others as compared to accusatory ones.[31]
- **"But" statements.** It's a good idea, *but* it won't work. You're really terrific, *but* I think we ought to spend less time together. (*But* cancels everything that went before the word.)
- **Questions versus statements.** Do you think we ought to do that? (less responsible) versus I don't think we ought to do that (more responsible).

Troublesome Language

Besides being a blessing that enables us to live together, language can be something of a curse. We have all known the frustration of being misunderstood, and most of us have been baffled by another person's overreaction to an innocent comment. In the following pages we will look at several kinds of troublesome language, with the goal of helping you communicate in a way that makes matters better instead of worse.

The Language of Misunderstandings

The most obvious kind of language problems are semantic: We simply don't understand others completely or accurately. Most misunderstandings arise from some common problems that are easily remedied—after you recognize them.

Equivocal Language   **Equivocal words** have more than one correct dictionary definition. Some equivocal misunderstandings are simple, at least after they are exposed. A nurse once told her patient that he "wouldn't be needing" the materials he requested from home. He interpreted the statement to mean he was near death when the nurse meant he would be going home soon. A colleague of ours mistakenly sent some confidential materials to the wrong person after his boss told him to "send them to

Richard," without specifying *which* Richard. Some equivocal misunderstandings can be embarrassing, as one woman recalls:

> In the fourth grade the teacher asked the class what a period was. I raised my hand and shared everything I had learned about girls' getting their period. But he was talking about the dot at the end of a sentence. Oops![32]

Equivocal misunderstandings can have serious consequences. Communication researchers Michael Motley and Heidi Reeder suggest that equivocation at least partially explains why men may sometimes persist in attempts to become physically intimate when women have expressed unwillingness to do so.[33] Interviews and focus groups with college students revealed that women often use ambiguous phrases to say "no" to a man's sexual advances: "I'm confused about this." "I'm not sure that we're ready for this yet." "Are you sure you want to do this?" "Let's be friends" and even "That tickles." (The researchers found that women were most likely to use less direct phrases when they hoped to see or date the man again. When they wanted to cut off the relationship, they were more likely to give a direct response.) Whereas women viewed indirect statements as equivalent to saying "no," men were more likely to interpret them as less clear-cut requests to stop. As the researchers put it, "male/female misunderstandings are not so much a matter of males hearing resistance messages as 'go,' but rather their not hearing them as 'stop.'" Under the law, "no" means precisely that, and anyone who argues otherwise can be in for serious legal problems.

Relative Words   **Relative words** gain their meaning by comparison. For example, is the school you attend large or small? This depends on what you compare it to: Alongside a campus like UCLA, with an enrollment of over thirty thousand students, it probably looks small, but compared to a smaller institution, it might seem quite large. In the same way, relative words like *fast* and *slow*, *smart* and *stupid*, *short* and *long* depend for their meaning upon what they're compared to. (The "large" size can of olives is the smallest you can buy; the larger ones are "giant," "colossal," and "supercolossal.")

Some relative words are so common that we mistakenly assume that they have a clear meaning. For instance, if a new acquaintance says "I'll call you soon," when can you expect to hear from him or her? In one study, graduate students were asked to assign numerical values to terms such as *doubtful*, *toss-up*, *likely*, *probable*, *good chance*, and *unlikely*.[34] There was a tremendous variation in the meaning of most of these terms. For example, the responses for *possible* ranged from 0 to 99 percent. *Good chance* meant between 35 and 90 percent, whereas *unlikely* fell between 0 and 40 percent.

Using relative words without explaining them can lead to communication problems. Have you ever responded to someone's question about the weather by saying it was warm, only to find out that what was warm to you was cold to the other person? Or have you followed a friend's advice and gone to a "cheap" restaurant, only to find that it was twice as expensive as you expected? Have you been disappointed to learn that classes you've heard were "easy" turned out to be hard, that journeys you were told would be "short" were long, that "unusual" ideas were really quite ordinary? The problem in each case came from failing to anchor the relative word used to a more precisely measurable word.

CULTURAL IDIOM
a period:
occurrence of menstruation

Slang and Jargon   **Slang** is language used by a group of people whose members belong to a similar co-culture or other group. Some slang is related to specialized interests and activities. For instance, cyclists who talk about "bonking" are referring to running out of energy. Rapsters know that "bling" refers to jewelry and a "whip" is a nice-looking car.

Other slang consists of *regionalisms*—terms that are understood by people who live in one geographic area but that are incomprehensible to outsiders. This sort of use illustrates how slang defines insiders and outsiders, creating a sense of identity and solidarity.[35] Residents of the fiftieth U.S. state know that when a fellow Alaskan says, "I'm going outside," he or she is leaving the state. In the East End of London, cockney dialect uses rhyming words as substitutes for everyday expressions: "bacon and eggs" for "legs," and "Barney Rubble" for "trouble." This sort of use also illustrates how slang can be used to identify insiders and outsiders: With enough shared rhyming, slang users could talk about outsiders without the clueless outsiders knowing that they were the subject of conversation ("Lovely set of bacons, eh?" "Stay away from him. He's Barney.").

Slang can also be age-related. Most college students know that drinkers wearing "beer goggles" have consumed enough alcohol that they find almost everyone of the opposite—or sometimes the same—sex attractive. At some schools, a "monkey" is the "other" woman or man in a boyfriend's or girlfriend's life: "I've heard Mitch is cheating on me. When I find his monkey, I'm gonna do her up!"[36]

Almost everyone uses some sort of **jargon:** the specialized vocabulary that functions as a kind of shorthand for people with common backgrounds and experience. Skateboarders have their own language to describe maneuvers: "ollie," "grind," and "shove it." Some jargon consists of *acronyms*—initials of terms that are combined to form a word. Stock traders refer to the NASDAQ (pronounced "naz-dak") securities index, and military people label failure to serve at one's post as being AWOL (absent without leave). The digital age has spawned its own vocabulary of jargon. For instance, computer users know that "viruses" are malicious programs that migrate from one computer to another, wreaking havoc. Likewise, "cookies" are tiny files that remote observers can use to monitor a user's computer habits. Some jargon goes beyond being descriptive and conveys attitudes. For example, cynics in the high-tech world sometimes refer to being fired from a job as being "uninstalled." They talk dismissively about the nonvirtual world as the "carbon community" and of books and newspapers as "treeware." Some technical support staffers talk of "banana problems," meaning those that could be figured out by monkeys, as in "This is a two-banana problem at worst."[37]

Jargon can be a valuable kind of shorthand for people who understand its use. The trauma team in a hospital emergency room can save time, and possibly lives, by speaking in shorthand, referring to "GSWs" (gunshot wounds), "chem 7" lab tests, and so on, but the same specialized vocabulary that works so well among insiders can mystify and confuse family members of the patient, who don't understand the jargon. The same sort of misunderstandings can arise in less critical settings when insiders use their own language with people who don't share the same vocabulary. Jeffrey Katzman of the William Morris Agency's Hollywood office experienced this sort of problem when he met with members of a Silicon Valley computer firm to discuss a joint project.

> When he used the phrase "in development," he meant a project that was as yet merely an idea. When the techies used it, on the other hand, they meant designing a specific game or program. Ultimately, says Katzman, he had to bring in a blackboard and literally define his terms. "It was like when the Japanese first came to Hollywood," he recalls. "They had to use interpreters, and we did too."[38]

CULTURAL IDIOM

techies:
computer experts

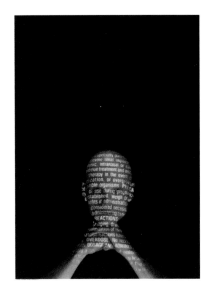

Overly Abstract Language Most objects, events, and ideas can be described with varying degrees of specificity. Consider the material you are reading. You could call it:

A book
A textbook
A communication textbook

Understanding Human Communication
Chapter 3 of *Understanding Human Communication*
Page 82 of Chapter 3 of *Understanding Human Communication*

In each case your description would be more and more specific. Semanticist S. I. Hayakawa created an **abstraction ladder** to describe this process.[39] This ladder consists of a number of descriptions of the same thing. Lower items focus specifically on the person, object, or event, whereas higher terms are generalizations that include the subject as a member of a larger class. To talk about "college," for example, is more abstract than to talk about a particular school.

Likewise, referring to "women" is more abstract than referring to "feminists," or more specifically naming feminist organizations or even specific members who belong to them.

Higher-level abstractions are a useful tool, because without them language would be too cumbersome to be useful. It's faster, easier, and more useful to talk about *Europe* than to list all of the countries on that continent. In the same way, using relatively abstract terms like *friendly* or *smart* can make it easier to describe people than listing their specific actions.

Abstract language—speech that refers to events or objects only vaguely—serves a second, less obvious function. At times it allows us to avoid confrontations by deliberately being unclear.[40] Suppose, for example, your boss is enthusiastic about a new approach to doing business that you think is a terrible idea. Telling the truth might seem too risky, but lying—saying "I think it's a great idea"—wouldn't feel right either. In situations like this an abstract answer can hint at your true belief without a direct confrontation: "I don't know . . . It's sure unusual . . . It *might* work." The same sort of abstract language can help you avoid embarrassing friends who ask for your opinion with questions like "What do you think of my new haircut?" An abstract response like "It's really different!" may be easier for you to deliver—and for your friend to receive—than the clear, brutal truth: "It's really ugly!" We will have more to say about this linguistic strategy of equivocation later in this chapter.

Although vagueness does have its uses, highly abstract language can cause several types of problems. The first is *stereotyping*. Consider claims like "All whites are bigots," "Men don't care about relationships," "The police are a bunch of goons," or "Professors around here care more about their research than they do about students." Each of these claims ignores the very important fact that abstract descriptions are almost always too general, that they say more than we really mean.

Besides creating stereotypical attitudes, abstract language can lead to the problem of *confusing others*. Imagine the lack of understanding that results from imprecise language in situations like this:

A: We never do anything that's fun anymore.

B: What do you mean?

A: We used to do lots of unusual things, but now it's the same old stuff, over and over.

CULTURAL IDIOM
goons:
those who intimidate others

B: But last week we went on that camping trip, and tomorrow we're going to that party where we'll meet all sorts of new people. Those are new things.

A: That's not what I mean. I'm talking about really unusual stuff.

B: *(becoming confused and a little impatient)* Like what? Taking hard drugs or going over Niagara Falls in a barrel?

A: Don't be stupid. All I'm saying is that we're in a rut. We should be living more exciting lives.

B: Well, I don't know what you want.

CULTURAL IDIOM

in a rut:
having fixed and monotonous
routines and habits

The best way to avoid this sort of overly abstract language is to use **behavioral descriptions** instead. (See Table 3-2.) Behavioral descriptions move down the abstraction ladder to identify the specific, observable phenomenon being discussed. A thorough description should answer three questions:

1. **Who Is Involved?** Are you speaking for just yourself or for others as well? Are you talking about a group of people ("the neighbors," "women") or specific individuals ("the people next door with the barking dog," "Lola and Lizzie")?

2. **In What Circumstances Does the Behavior Occur?** Where does it occur: everywhere or in specific places (at parties, at work, in public)? When does it occur: When you're tired or when a certain subject comes up? The behavior you are describing probably doesn't occur all the time. In order to be understood, you need to pin down what circumstances set this situation apart from other ones.

TABLE 3-2   Abstract and Behavioral Descriptions

		Behavioral Description			
	Abstract Description	Who Is Involved	In What Circumstances	Specific Behaviors	Remarks
Problem	I talk too much	People I find intimidating	When I want them to like me	I talk (mostly about myself) instead of giving them a chance to speak or asking about their lives.	Behavioral description more clearly identifies behaviors to change.
Goal	I want to be more constructive.	My roommate	When we talk about household duties	Instead of finding fault with her ideas, suggest alternatives that might work.	Behavioral description clearly outlines how to act; abstract description doesn't.
Appreciation	"You're really been helpful lately."	(Deliver to fellow workers)	"When I've had to take time off work because of personal problems"	"You took my shifts without complaining."	Give both abstract and behavioral descriptions for best results.
Request	"Clean up your act!"	(Deliver to target person)	"When we're around my family"	"Please don't tell jokes that involve sex."	Behavioral description specifies desired behavior.

3. **What Behaviors Are Involved?** Though terms such as *more cooperative* and *helpful* might sound like concrete descriptions of behavior, they are usually too vague to do a clear job of explaining what's on your mind. Behaviors must be *observable*, ideally both to you and to others. For instance, moving down the abstraction ladder from the relatively vague term *helpful*, you might come to behaviors such as *does the dishes every other day, volunteers to help me with my studies*, or *fixes dinner once or twice a week without being asked*. It's easy to see that terms like these are easier for both you and others to understand than are more vague abstractions.

Behavioral descriptions can improve communication in a wide range of situations, as Table 3-2 illustrates. Research also supports the value of specific language. One study found that well-adjusted couples had just as many conflicts as poorly adjusted couples, but the way the well-adjusted couples handled their problems was significantly different. Instead of blaming one another, the well-adjusted couples expressed their complaints in behavioral terms.[41] For instance, instead of saying "You're a slob," an enlightened partner might say, "I wish you wouldn't leave your dishes in the sink."

Disruptive Language

Not all linguistic problems come from misunderstandings. Sometimes people understand one another perfectly and still end up in conflict. Of course, not all disagreements can, or should be, avoided. But eliminating three bad linguistic habits from your communication repertoire can minimize the kind of clashes that don't need to happen, allowing you to save your energy for the unavoidable and important struggles.

Confusing Facts and Opinions

Factual statements are claims that can be verified as true or false. By contrast, **opinion statements** are based on the speaker's beliefs. Unlike matters of fact, they can never be proved or disproved. Consider a few examples of the difference between factual statements and opinion statements:

FACT	OPINION
It rains more in Seattle than in Portland.	The climate in Portland is better than in Seattle.
Kareem Abdul Jabbar is the all-time leading scorer in the National Basketball Association.	Kareem is the greatest basketball player in the history of the game.
Per capita income in the United States is lower than in several other countries.	The United States is not the best model of economic success in the world.

When factual statements and opinion statements are set side by side like this, the difference between them is clear. In everyday conversation, we often present our opinions as if they were facts, and in doing so we invite an unnecessary argument. For example:

- "That was a dumb thing to say!"
- "Spending that much on _____ is a waste of money!"
- "You can't get a fair shake in this country unless you're a white male."

Notice how much less antagonistic each statement would be if it was prefaced by a qualifier like "In my opinion . . ." or "It seems to me . . . ."

Confusing Facts and Inferences

Labeling your opinions can go a long way toward relational harmony, but developing this habit won't solve all linguistic problems. Dif-

CULTURAL IDIOM
a fair shake:
honest treatment

ficulties also arise when we confuse factual statements with **inferential statements**—conclusions arrived at from an interpretation of evidence. Consider a few examples:

CULTURAL IDIOM

to weasel out of:
to get out of doing something

FACT	INFERENCE
He hit a lamppost while driving down the street.	He was daydreaming when he hit the lamppost.
You interrupted me before I finished what I was saying.	You don't care about what I have to say.
You haven't paid your share of the rent on time for the past three months.	You're trying to weasel out of your responsibilities.
I haven't gotten a raise in almost a year.	The boss is exploiting me.

There's nothing wrong with making inferences as long as you identify them as such: "She stomped out and slammed the door. It looked to me as if she were furious." The danger comes when we confuse inferences with facts and make them sound like the absolute truth.

One way to avoid fact-inference confusion is to use the perception-checking skill described in Chapter 2 to test the accuracy of your inferences. Recall that a perception check has three parts: a description of the behavior being discussed, your interpretation of that behavior, and a request for verification. For instance, instead of saying "Why are you laughing at me?" you could say, "When you laugh like that *[description of behavior]*, I get the idea you think something I did was stupid *[interpretation]*. Are you laughing at me *[question]*?"

Emotive Language **Emotive language** contains words that sound as if they're describing something when they are really announcing the speaker's attitude toward something. Do you like that old picture frame? If so, you would probably call it "an antique," but if you think it's ugly, you would likely describe it as "a piece of junk." Emotive words may sound like statements of fact but are always opinions.

Barbra Streisand pointed out how some people use emotive language to stigmatize behavior in women that they admire in men:

A man is commanding—a woman is demanding.
A man is forceful—a woman is pushy.
A man is uncompromising—a woman is a ball-breaker.
A man is a perfectionist—a woman's a pain in the ass.
He's assertive—she's aggressive.
He strategizes—she manipulates.
He shows leadership—she's controlling.
He's committed—she's obsessed.
He's persevering—she's relentless.
He sticks to his guns—she's stubborn.
If a man wants to get it right, he's looked up to and respected.
If a woman wants to get it right, she's difficult and impossible.[42]

The reading on page 87 illustrates how emotive language can escalate conflicts and make constructive dialogue difficult, or even impossible.

As this reading suggests, problems occur when people use emotive words without labeling them as such. You might, for instance, have a long and bitter argument with a friend about whether a third person

Source: Candorville. Washington Post Writer's Group.

was "assertive" or "obnoxious," when a more accurate and peaceable way to handle the issue would be to acknowledge that one of you approves of the behavior and the other doesn't.

CRITICAL THINKING PROBE

● Emotive Language

Test your ability to identify emotive language by playing the following word game.

1. Take an action, object, or characteristic and show how it can be viewed either favorably or unfavorably, according to the label it is given. For example:

   a. I'm casual.

      You're careless.

      He's a slob.

   b. I read adult love stories.

      You read erotic literature.

      She reads pornography.

2. Now create three-part descriptions of your own, using the following statements as a start:

   a. I'm tactful.

   b. She's a liar.

   c. I'm conservative.

   d. You have a high opinion of yourself.

   e. I'm quiet.

   f. You're pessimistic.

3. Now recall two situations in which you used emotive language as if it were a description of fact. How might the results have differed if you had used more objective language?

Evasive Language

None of the troublesome language habits we have described so far is a deliberate strategy to mislead or antagonize others. Now, however, we'll consider euphemisms and equivocations, two types of language that speakers use by design to avoid communicating clearly. Although both of these have some very legitimate uses, they also can lead to frustration and confusion.

Euphemisms   A **euphemism** (from the Greek word meaning "to use words of good omen") is a pleasant term substituted for a more direct but potentially less pleasant one. We are using euphemisms when we say "restroom" instead of "toilet" or "full-figured" instead of "overweight." There certainly are cases where the euphemistic pulling of linguistic punches can be face-saving. It's probably more constructive to question a possible "statistical misrepresentation" than to call someone a liar, for example. Likewise, it may be less disquieting to some to refer to people as "senior citizens" than "old."

Like many businesses, the airline industry uses euphemisms to avoid upsetting already nervous flyers.[43] For example, rather than saying "turbulence," pilots and flight attendants use the less frightening term "bumpy air." Likewise, they refer to thunderstorms as "rain showers," and fog as "mist" or "haze." And savvy flight personnel never use the words "your final destination."

INVITATION TO INSIGHT
Becoming Desensitized to Hate Words

The ceremonies are over, but I would like to suggest one last way to commemorate the golden anniversary of the defeat of the Nazis. How about a moratorium on the current abuse of terms like storm trooper, swastika, Holocaust, Gestapo, and Hitler? How about putting the language of the Third Reich into mothballs?

The further we are removed from the defeat of the Nazis, the more this vocabulary seems to be taking over our own. It's become part of the casual, ubiquitous, inflammatory speech Americans use to turn each other into monsters. Which, if I recall correctly, was a tactic favored by Goebbels himself.

The NRA attacked federal agents as "jackbooted government thugs who wear Nazi bucket helmets and black storm trooper uniforms." In the ratcheting up of the rhetorical wars, it wasn't enough for the NRA to complain that the agents had overstepped their bounds; they had to call them Nazis.

Republican congressmen have compared environmentalist agencies with Hitler's troops. Pennsylvania's Bud Shuster talked about EPA officials as an "environmental Gestapo." Missouri's Bill Emerson warned about the establishment of an "eco-Gestapo force."

On the Democratic side, Sen. John Kerry recently suggested that a proposed new kind of tax audit, on "lifestyles," would produce an "IRS Gestapo-like entity." And John Lewis and Charles Rangel compared silence in the face of the new conservative agenda to silence in the early days of the Third Reich. They didn't just disagree with conservatives; they Nazified them.

Then there are the perennial entries on the Hitler log. Anti-abortion groups talk about the abortion holocaust—comparing the fetuses to Jews and the doctors to Mengele. As for pinning the Nazi label on supporters of abortion rights, the propagandists surely know that Hitler was a hard-line opponent of abortion. (Did that make him pro life?)

Even when Nazi-speak isn't historically dumb, it's rhetorically dumb. The Hitlerian language has become indiscriminate shorthand for every petty tyranny. In this vocabulary, every two-bit boss becomes a "little Hitler." Every domineering high school principal is accused of running a "concentration camp." Every overbearing piece of behavior becomes a "Gestapo" tactic. And every political disagreement becomes a fight against evil.

Crying Hitler in our time is like crying wolf. The charge immediately escalates the argument, adding verbal fuel to fires of any dimension, however minor. But eventually, yelling Nazi at environmentalists and Gestapo at federal agents diminishes the emotional power of these words should we need them. In time, these epithets even downgrade the horror of the Third Reich and the immensity of World War II. They cheapen history and insult memory, especially the memory of the survivors.

Fifty years ago, Americans learned, with a fresh sense of horror, about the crematoriums, about man's inhumanity, about the trains that ran on time to the gas chambers. This was Nazism. This was the Gestapo. This was the Holocaust. This was Hitler. If you please, save the real words for the real thing.

Ellen Goodman

Despite their occasional advantages, many euphemisms are not worth the effort it takes to create them. Some are pretentious and confusing, such as a middle school's labeling of hallways as "behavior transition corridors." Other euphemisms are downright deceptive, such as the U.S. Senate's labeling of a $23,200 pay raise a "pay equalization concept."

Equivocation   It's 8:15 P.M., and you are already a half-hour late for your dinner reservation at the fanciest restaurant in town. Your partner has finally finished dressing and confronts you with the question "How do I look?" To tell the truth, you hate your partner's outfit. You don't want to lie, but on the other hand you don't want to be hurtful. Just as importantly, you don't want to lose your table by waiting around for your date to choose something else to wear. You think for a moment and then reply, "You look amazing. I've never seen an outfit like that before. Where did you get it?"

Your response in this situation was an **equivocation**—a deliberately vague statement that can be interpreted in more than one way. Earlier in this chapter we talked

CULTURAL IDIOM

putting . . . into mothballs:
retiring

two-bit:
unimportant, minor

crying wolf:
issuing a false alarm

"Be honest with me Roger. By 'mid-course correction' you mean divorce, don't you."

about how *unintentional* equivocation can lead to misunderstandings. But our discussion here focuses on *intentionally ambiguous speech* that is used to avoid lying on one hand and telling a painful truth on the other. Equivocations have several advantages. They spare the receiver from the embarrassment that might come from a completely truthful answer, and it can be easier for the sender to equivocate than to suffer the discomfort of being honest.

Despite its benefits, there are times when communicators equivocate as a way to weasel out of delivering important but unpleasant messages. Suppose, for example, that you are unsure about your standing in one of your courses. You approach the professor and ask how you're doing. "Not bad," the professor answers. This answer isn't too satisfying. "What grade am I earning?" you inquire. "Oh, lots of people would be happy with it" is the answer you receive. "But will I receive an A or B this semester?" you persist. "You *could*," is the reply. It's easy to see how this sort of evasiveness can be frustrating.

As with euphemisms, high-level abstractions, and many other types of communication, it's impossible to say that equivocation is always helpful or harmful. As you learned in Chapter 1, competent communication behavior is situational. Your success in relating to others will depend on your ability to analyze yourself, the other person, and the situation when deciding whether to be equivocal or direct.

ETHICAL CHALLENGE

● **Euphemisms and Equivocations**

For most people, "telling it like it is" is usually considered a virtue and "beating around the bush" is a minor sin. You can test the function of indirect speech by following these directions:

1. Identify five examples of euphemisms and equivocations in everyday interaction.
2. Imagine how matters would have been different if the speakers or writers had used direct language in each situation.
3. Based on your observations, discuss whether equivocation and euphemisms have any place in face-to-face communication.

Gender and Language

So far we have discussed language use as if it were identical for both sexes. Some theorists and researchers, though, have argued that there are significant differences between the way men and women speak, whereas others have argued that any differences are not significant.[44] What are the similarities and differences between male and female language use?

Content

Although there is a great deal of variation within each gender, on the average, men and women discuss a surprisingly different range of topics. The first research on conversational topics was conducted over seventy years ago. Despite the changes in male and female roles since then, the results of more recent studies are remarkably similar.[45] In these studies, women and men ranging in age from seventeen to eighty described the range of topics each discussed with friends of the same sex. Certain topics were common to both sexes: work, movies, and television proved to be frequent for both groups. Both men and women reserved discussions of sex and sexuality for members of the same gender. The differences between men and women were more striking than the similarities, however. Female friends spent much more time discussing personal and domestic subjects, relationship problems, family, health and reproductive matters, weight, food and clothing, men, and other women. Men, on the other hand, were more likely to discuss music, current events, sports, business, and other men. Both men and women were equally likely to discuss personal appearance, sex, and dating in same-sex conversations. True to one common stereotype, women were more likely to gossip about close friends and family. By contrast, men spent more time gossiping about sports figures and media personalities. Women's gossip was no more derogatory than men's.

These differences can lead to frustration when men and women try to converse with one another. Researchers report that *trivial* is the word often used by both sexes to describe topics discussed by the opposite sex.

Reasons for Communicating

Research shows that the notion that men and women communicate in dramatically different ways is exaggerated. Both men and women, at least in the dominant cultures of the United States and Canada, use language to build and maintain social relationships.[46] *How* men and women accomplish these goals is often different, though. Although most communicators try to make their interaction enjoyable, men are more likely than women to emphasize making conversation fun. Their discussions involve a greater amount of joking and good-natured teasing. By contrast, women's conversations focus more frequently on feelings, relationships, and personal problems. In fact, communication researcher Julia Wood flatly states that "for women, talk *is* the essence of relationships."[47] When a group of women was surveyed to find out what kinds of satisfaction they gained from talking with their friends, the most common theme mentioned was a feeling of empathy—"To know you're not alone," as some put it. [48] Whereas men commonly described same-sex conversations as something they *liked*, women characterized their woman-to-woman talks as a kind of contact they *needed*. The greater frequency of female conversations reflects their importance. Nearly 50 percent of the women surveyed said they called friends at least once a week just to talk, whereas less than half as many men did so. In fact, 40 percent of the men surveyed reported that they never called another man just to talk.

Because women use conversation to pursue social needs, female speech typically contains statements showing support for the other person, demonstrations of equality, and efforts to keep the conversation going. With these goals, it's not surprising that traditionally female speech often contains statements of sympathy and empathy: "I've felt just like that myself," "The same thing happened to me!" Women are also inclined to ask lots of questions that invite the other person to share information: "How did you feel about that?" "What did you do next?" The importance of nurturing a relationship also explains why female speech is often somewhat powerless and tentative. Saying, "This is just my opinion . . ." is less likely to put off a conversational partner than a more definite "Here's what I think . . . ."

CULTURAL IDIOM

one-up:
respond in order to maintain one's
superiority

Men's speech is often driven by quite different goals than women's. Men are more likely to use language to accomplish the job at hand than to nourish relationships. This explains why men are less likely than women to disclose their vulnerabilities, which would be a sign of weakness. When someone else is sharing a problem, instead of empathizing, men are prone to offer advice: "That's nothing to worry about . . ." or "Here's what you need to do . . . ." Besides taking care of business, men are more likely than women to use conversations to exert control, preserve their independence, and enhance their status. This explains why men are more prone to dominate conversations and one-up their partners. Men interrupt their conversational partners to assert their own experiences or point of view. (Women interrupt too, but they usually do so to offer support: quite a different goal.) Just because male talk is competitive doesn't mean it's not enjoyable. Men often regard talk as a kind of game: When researchers asked men what they liked best about their all-male talk, the most frequent answer was its ease.[49] Another common theme was appreciation of the practical value of conversation: new ways to solve problems. Men also mentioned enjoying the humor and rapid pace that characterized their all-male conversations.

Conversational Style

Some scholarship shows little difference between the ways men and women converse. For example, the popular myth that women are more talkative than men may not be accurate. Researchers found that men and women speak roughly the same number of words per day.[50]

On the other hand, there are ways in which women do behave differently in conversations than do men.[51] For example, women ask more questions in mixed-sex conversations than do men—nearly three times as many, according to one study. Other research has revealed that in mixed-sex conversations, men interrupt women far more than the other way around. Some theorists have argued that differences like these result in women's speech that is less powerful and more emotional than men's. Research has supported these theories—at least in some cases. Even when clues about the speakers' sex were edited out, raters found clear differences between transcripts of male speech and female speech. In one study women's talk was judged more aesthetic, whereas men's talk was seen as more dynamic, aggressive, and strong. In another, male job applicants were rated more fluent, active, confident, and effective than female applicants.

Given these differences, it's easy to wonder how men and women manage to communicate with one another at all. One reason why cross-sex conversations do run smoothly is because women accommodate to the topics men raise. Both men and women regard topics introduced by women as tentative, whereas topics that men introduce are more likely to be pursued. Thus, women seem to grease the wheels of conversation by doing more work than men in maintaining conversations. A complementary difference between men and women also promotes cross-sex conversations: Men are more likely to talk about themselves with women than with other men, and

CULTURAL IDIOM

to grease the wheels:
to facilitate

because women are willing to adapt to this topic, conversations are likely to run smoothly, if one-sidedly.

An accommodating style isn't always a disadvantage for women. One study revealed that women who spoke tentatively were actually more influential with men than those who used more powerful speech.[52] On the other hand, this tentative style was less effective in persuading women. (Language use had no effect on men's persuasiveness.) This research suggests that women who are willing and able to be flexible in their approach can persuade both other women and men—as long as they are not dealing with a mixed-sex audience.

Nongender Variables

Despite the differences in the ways men and women speak, the link between gender and language use isn't as clear-cut as it might seem. Research reviews have found that the ways women and men communicate are much more similar than different. For example, one analysis of over twelve hundred research studies found that only 1 percent of variance in communication behavior resulted from sex difference.[53] There is no significant difference between male speech and female speech in areas such as use of profanity, use of qualifiers such as "I guess" or "This is just my opinion," tag questions, and vocal fluency.[54] Some on-the-job research shows that male and female supervisors in similar positions behave the same way and are equally effective. In light of the considerable similarities between the sexes and the relatively minor differences, some communication scholars suggest that the "men are from Mars, women are from Venus" claim should be replaced by the metaphor that "men are from North Dakota, women are from South Dakota."[55]

A growing body of research explains some of the apparent contradictions between the similarities and differences between male speech and female speech. They have revealed other factors that influence language use as much or more than does gender. For example, social philosophy plays a role. Feminist wives talk longer than their partners, whereas nonfeminist wives speak less than their husbands. Orientation toward problem solving also plays a role in conversational style. The cooperative or competitive orientations of speakers have more influence on how they interact than does their gender.

The speaker's occupation and social role also influence speaking style. For example, male day-care teachers' speech to their students resembles the language of female teachers more closely than it resembles the language of fathers at home. Overall, doctors interrupt their patients more often than the reverse, although male patients do interrupt female physicians more often than their male counterparts. At work, task differences exert more powerful effects on whether speakers use gender-inclusive language (such as "he or she" instead of just "he") than does biological sex.[56] A close study of trial transcripts showed that the speaker's experience on the witness stand and occupation had more to do with language use than did gender. If women generally use "powerless" language, this may possibly reflect their historical social role in society at large. As the balance of power grows more equal between men and women, we can expect many linguistic differences to shrink.

Another powerful force that influences the way individual men and women speak is their **sex role**—the social orientation that governs behavior—rather than their biological gender. Researchers have identified three sex roles: masculine, feminine, and androgynous. These sex roles don't always line up neatly with gender. There are "masculine" females, "feminine" males, and androgynous communicators who combine traditionally masculine and feminine characteristics.

Research shows that linguistic differences are often a function of these sex roles more than the speaker's biological sex. Masculine sex-role communicators—whether male or female—use more dominant language than either feminine or androgynous speakers. Feminine speakers have the most submissive speaking style, whereas androgynous speakers fall between these extremes. When two masculine communicators are in a conversation, they often engage in a one-up battle for dominance, responding to the other's bid for control with a counterattempt to dominate the relationship. Feminine sex-role speakers are less predictable. They use dominance, submission, and equivalent behavior in an almost random fashion. Androgynous individuals are more predictable: They most frequently meet another's bid for dominance with a symmetrical attempt at control, but then move quickly toward an equivalent relationship.

All this information suggests that, when it comes to communicating, "masculinity" and "femininity" are culturally recognized sex roles, not biological traits. Research suggests that neither a stereotypically male style nor female style is the best choice. For example, one study showed that a "mixed-gender strategy" that balanced the stereotypically male task-oriented approach with the stereotypically female relationship-oriented approach received the highest marks by both male and female respondents.[57] As opportunities for men and women become more equal, we can expect that the differences between male and female use of language will become smaller.

Culture and Language

Anyone who has tried to translate ideas from one language to another knows that communication across cultures can be a challenge.[58] Sometimes the results of a bungled translation can be amusing. For example, the American manufacturers of Pet condensed milk unknowingly introduced their product in French-speaking markets without realizing that the word *pet* in French means "to break wind."[59] Likewise, the naive English-speaking representative of a U.S. soft drink manufacturer drew laughs from Mexican customers when she offered free samples of Fresca soda pop. In Mexican slang, the word *fresca* means "lesbian."

Even choosing the right words during translation won't guarantee that nonnative speakers will use an unfamiliar language correctly. For example, Japanese insurance companies warn their policyholders who are visiting the United States to avoid their cultural tendency to say "excuse me" or "I'm sorry" if they are involved in a traffic accident.[60]

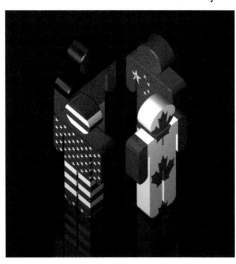

In Japan, apologizing is a traditional way to express goodwill and maintain social harmony, even if the person offering the apology is not at fault. But in the United States, an apology can be taken as an admission of guilt and may result in Japanese tourists' being held accountable for accidents for which they may not be responsible.

Difficult as it may be, translation is only a small part of the communication challenges facing members of different cultures. Differences in the way language is used and the very worldview that a language creates make communicating across cultures a challenging task.

Verbal Communication Styles

Using language is more than just choosing a particular group of words to convey an idea. Each language has its own unique style that distinguishes it from others. And when a communicator tries to use the verbal style from one culture in a different one, problems are likely to arise.[61]

Direct–Indirect   One way in which verbal styles vary is in their *directness*. Anthropologist Edward Hall identified two distinct cultural ways of using language.[62] **Low-context cultures** use language primarily to express thoughts, feelings, and ideas as clearly and logically as possible. To low-context communicators, the meaning of a statement is in the words spoken. By contrast, **high-context cultures** value language as a way to maintain social harmony. Rather than upset others by speaking clearly, communicators in these cultures learn to discover meaning from the context in which a message is delivered: the nonverbal behaviors of the speaker, the history of the relationship, and the general social rules that govern interaction between people. Table 3-3 summarizes some key differences between the way low- and high-context cultures use language.

North American culture falls toward the direct, low-context end of the scale. Residents of the United States and Canada value straight talk and grow impatient with "beating around the bush." By contrast, most Asian and Middle Eastern cultures fit the high-context pattern. In many Asian cultures, for example, maintaining harmony is important, and so communicators will avoid speaking directly if that would threaten another person's face. For this reason, Japanese or Koreans are less likely than Americans to offer a clear "no" to an undesirable request. Instead, they would probably use roundabout expressions like "I agree with you in principle, but . . ." or "I sympathize with you . . . ."

Low-context North Americans may miss the subtleties of high-context messages, but people raised to recognize indirect communication have little trouble decoding them. A look at Japanese child-rearing practices helps explain why. Research shows that Japanese mothers rarely deny the requests of their young children by saying "no." Instead, they use other strategies: ignoring a child's requests, raising distractions, promising to take care of the matter later, or explaining why they can or will not say "yes."[63] Sociolinguist Deborah Tannen explains how this indirect approach illustrates profound differences between high- and low-context communication:

> . . . saying no is something associated with children who have not yet learned the norm. If a Japanese mother spoke that way, she would feel she was lowering herself to her child's level precisely because that way of speaking is associated with Japanese children.[64]

CULTURAL IDIOM
"beating around the bush": approaching something in an indirect way

TABLE 3-3   Low- and High-Context Communication Styles

Low Context	High Context
Majority of information carried in explicit verbal messages, with less focus on the situational context.	Important information carried in contextual clues (time, place, relationship, situation). Less reliance on explicit verbal messages.
Self-expression valued. Communicators state opinions and desires directly and strive to persuade others.	Relational harmony valued and maintained by indirect expression of opinions. Communicators refrain from saying "no" directly.
Clear, eloquent speech considered praiseworthy. Verbal fluency admired.	Communicators talk "around" the point, allowing others to fill in the missing pieces. Ambiguity and use of silence admired.

"You seem familiar, yet somehow strange—are you by any chance Canadian?"

Tannen goes on to contrast the Japanese notion of appropriateness with the very different one held by dominant North American society:

> Because American norms for talk are different, it is common, and therefore expected, for American parents to "just say no." That's why an American mother feels authoritative when she talks that way: because it fits her image of how an authoritative adult talks to a child.[65]

The clash between cultural norms of directness and indirectness can aggravate problems in cross-cultural situations such as encounters between straight-talking low-context Israelis, who value speaking directly, and Arabs, whose high-context culture stresses smooth interaction. It's easy to imagine how the clash of cultural styles could lead to misunderstandings and conflicts between Israelis and their Palestinian neighbors. Israelis could view their Arab counterparts as evasive, whereas the Palestinians could perceive the Israelis as insensitive and blunt.

Even within a single country, subcultures can have different notions about the value of direct speech. For example, Puerto Rican language style resembles high-context Japanese or Korean more than low-context English.[66] As a group, Puerto Ricans value social harmony and avoid confrontation, which leads them to systematically speak in an indirect way to avoid giving offense. Asian Americans are more offended by indirectly racist statements than are African Americans, Hispanics, and Anglo Americans.[67] Researchers Laura Leets and Howard Giles suggest that the traditional Asian tendency to favor high-context messages explains the difference: Adept at recognizing hints and nonverbal cues, high-context communicators are more sensitive to messages that are overlooked by people from cultural groups that rely more heavily on unambiguous, explicit low-context messages.

It's worth noting that even generally straight-talking residents of the United States raised in the low-context Euro-American tradition often rely on context to make their point. When you decline an unwanted invitation by saying "I can't make it," it's likely that both you and the other person know that the choice of attending isn't really beyond your control. If your goal was to be perfectly clear, you might say, "I don't want to get together."

Elaborate–Succinct   Another way in which language styles can vary across cultures is in terms of whether they are *elaborate* or *succinct*. Speakers of Arabic, for instance, commonly use language that is much more rich and expressive than most communicators who use English. Strong assertions and exaggerations that would sound ridiculous in English are a common feature of Arabic. This contrast in linguistic style can lead to misunderstandings between people from different backgrounds. As one observer put it,

> . . . [A]n Arab feels compelled to overassert in almost all types of communication because others expect him [or her] to. If an Arab says exactly what he [or she] means without the expected assertion, other Arabs may still think that he [or she] means the opposite. For example, a simple "no" to a host's requests to eat more or drink more will not suffice. To convey the meaning that he [or she] is actually full, the guest must keep repeating "no" several times, coupling it with an oath such as "By God" or "I swear to God."[68]

Succinctness is most extreme in cultures where silence is valued. In many American Indian cultures, for example, the favored way to handle ambiguous social situations is to remain quiet.[69] When you contrast this silent style to the talkativeness common in mainstream American cultures when people first meet, it's easy to imagine how the first encounter between an Apache or Navajo and a white person might feel uncomfortable to both people.

UNDERSTANDING DIVERSITY

European Languages Keep Watch on "You"

In continental Europe it's all about you. Or rather, tu. Or vous. Or u or jij. Or ty or vy.

Here, addressing a person in the singular or plural is more than just a question of grammar, it's a social minefield. In France it can be a matter of state. A misused "vous" can make you seem cold or snobbish. But use "tu" to an elder or a boss and you risk being accused of acting overly familiar, or insolently.

The rules are wavering a bit under the onslaught of the class-busting Internet, irreverent TV hosts, the influence of English and modernity's generally more relaxed ways. But from Paris to St. Petersburg, Bologna to Budapest and into the non-English-speaking New World beyond, using the wrong form of "you" can cause great offense—a sort of verbal poke in the eye.

Simply put, European languages that break "you" down into several different forms do so depending on who the speaker is addressing. It is what linguists call a "T-V distinction," distinguishing formal and informal ways of saying "you."

In general, Europeans use the informal singular ("tu" in French and Italian, "jij" in Dutch, "ty" in Russian) when speaking to children, close family and friends, and a formal version ("vous," "u," "vy") for everyone else, especially the elderly or people otherwise deserving of respect.

Sounds simple? Well, yes and no. Exceptions to the rules are endless.

The wife of former French President Jacques Chirac, Bernadette, says she simply does not care for the informality of "tu." So even after 50 years of marriage the couple still address each other with the formal "vous."

In Russia, some police and military officers like to assert their authority by deliberately using the informal "ty" when making arrests or pulling over motorists. Such verbal manhandling can draw a rebuke: "Ne tyky"—Don't call me "ty."

Some non-native Russian-speakers prefer the formal because they find its verb forms easier to conjugate, but that too can be a problem, because it can sound as though the speaker is distancing himself from whomever he is addressing.

In Paris, Australian Katia Grimmer-Laversanne (she met her French husband over the Internet; they did their electronic courting in English), likes to let new acquaintances take the lead.

If they leap straight in with "tu," then she knows that it's OK to be informal back.

"I prefer that they set the ground rules rather than me, because I have had so many embarrassing situations," says the 26-year-old graphic designer. "In English, whether you're speaking to your best friend or the prime minister of Australia, it really doesn't matter how you say 'How are you?' But living here, it's a whole different ball game."

In professional and other contexts, "vous" can be useful in keeping a relationship at arm's length. Psychiatrists may use "vous" lest the relationship with the patient get too close. Some reporters use "vous" to politicians they have known for years, just to preserve their objectivity.

"There is a whole art to the use of 'vous' and 'tu.' They transmit a wealth of values," said Marceau Dechamps, whose group, the Defense of the French Language, campaigns to protect French from the creeping influence of English, which shed "thou" centuries ago.

Dechamps, the group's vice president, said he personally would favor simplifying French to make it "more logical, more coherent." But ditch the tu-vous distinction? "Ah, non!" he exclaimed.

Doing so, he noted, would rob French-speakers of that magic moment when they decide that someone they have long addressed as "vous" has become close enough to be worthy of a "tu"—like the waiter who, after years of serving your morning cafe creme, declares out of the blue: "Monsieur, after all this time, I think we can use 'tu' with each other."

"It is the passage from acquaintance to love," said Dechamps. "It is a marker."

Kentucky Enquirer, March 5, 2006, Section A, Page 17. John Leicester, Associated Press. Retrieved from http://mdn.mainichi-msn .co.jp/features/news/20060302p2g00m0fe012000c.html.

Formal–Informal Along with differences such as directness-indirectness and elaborate-succinct styles, a third way languages differ from one culture to another involves *formality* and *informality*. The informal approach that characterizes relationships in countries like the United States, Canada, and Australia is quite different from the great concern for using proper speech in many parts of Asia and Africa. Formality isn't so

CULTURAL IDIOM

tongue:
language

much a matter of using correct grammar as of defining social position. In Korea, for example, the language reflects the Confucian system of relational hierarchies.[70] It has special vocabularies for different sexes, for different levels of social status, for different degrees of intimacy, and for different types of social occasions. For example, there are different degrees of formality for speaking with old friends, nonacquaintances whose background one knows, and complete strangers. One sign of being a learned person in Korea is the ability to use language that recognizes these relational distinctions. When you contrast these sorts of distinctions with the casual friendliness many North Americans use even when talking with complete strangers, it's easy to see how a Korean might view communicators in the United States as boorish and how an American might view Koreans as stiff and unfriendly.

Language and Worldview

Different linguistic styles are important, but there may be even more fundamental differences that separate speakers of various languages. For almost 150 years, some theorists have put forth the notion of **linguistic relativism:** the notion that the worldview of a culture is shaped and reflected by the language its members speak. The best-known example of linguistic relativism is the notion that Eskimos have a large number of words (estimated from seventeen to one hundred) for what we simply call "snow." Different terms are used to describe conditions like a driving blizzard, crusty ice, and light powder. This example suggests how linguistic determinism operates. The need to survive in an Arctic environment led Eskimos to make distinctions that would be unimportant to residents of warmer environments, and after the language makes these distinctions, speakers are more likely to see the world in ways that match the broader vocabulary.

Even though there is some doubt that Eskimos really do have one hundred words for snow,[71] other examples do seem to support the principle of linguistic relativism.[72] For instance, bilingual speakers seem to think differently when they change languages. In one study, French Americans were asked to interpret a series of pictures. When they spoke in French, their descriptions were far more romantic and emotional than when they used English to describe the same kind of pictures. Likewise, when students in Hong Kong were asked to complete a values test, they expressed more traditional Chinese values when they answered in Cantonese than when they answered in English.

In Israel, both Arab and Jewish students saw bigger distinctions between their group and "outsiders" when using their native language than when they used English, a neutral tongue. Examples like these show the power of language to shape cultural identity—sometimes for better and sometimes for worse.

Linguistic influences start early in life. English-speaking parents often label the mischievous pranks of their children as "bad," implying that there is something immoral about acting wild. "Be good!" they are inclined to say. On the other hand, French parents are more likely to say *"Sois sage!"*—"Be wise." The linguistic implication is that misbehaving is an act of foolishness. Swedes would correct the same action with the words *"Var snall!"*—"Be friendly, be kind." By contrast, German adults would use the command *"Sei artig!"*—literally, "Be of your own kind"—in other words, get back in step, conform to your role as a child.[73]

"The Eskimos have eighty-seven words for snow and not one for malpractice."

INVITATION TO INSIGHT
When Words Hurt

Words are scalpels, every bit as sharp as a surgeon's tools, and sometimes almost as dangerous.

Cutting words are at their worst when they are unintended, that is, when they inadvertently reveal what the speaker—the doctor—really thinks. Take "incompetent cervix." Granted, this is a succinct way to describe a cervix that can't keep the womb properly closed throughout a pregnancy. But we never hear the term "incompetent penis."

Far worse is the common phrase, "The patient failed chemotherapy." Who or what really failed here? "The therapy failed the patient" is not only kinder but more accurate.

Another alienating word is "denies," as in, "the patient denies alcohol use" or "the patient has cough but denies phlegm." Sure, it lets one doctor know that another has asked a patient about this, but the not-so-hidden connotation is that the patient is a liar.

As a much-published poet, Dr. Rafael Campo, a primary care physician at Beth Israel Deaconess Medical Center in Boston, is attuned to the potential damage—and the healing power—of words.

"Some of the language we are talking about here is pervasive in the medical profession and does potentially undermine the relationship between doctors and patients," he says.

For example, doctors often say the patient came in "complaining of" something, which makes the patient sound whiny, like "an adversary," Campo says. "Just the other day, an intern was presenting a patient [to me] in front of the patient. He said, 'Mrs. So and So is here complaining of . . .' and she said, 'I wasn't complaining, I was just telling you how I feel.'"

Says Campo, the author of *The Healing Art: A Doctor's Black Bag of Poetry*. "There is no handbook for medicalese that says we have to talk in these terms. . . . But it's this kind of short-hand formulas that gets passed down from one generation of doctors to the next."

Judy Foreman

The best-known declaration of linguistic relativism is the **Sapir-Whorf hypothesis,** formulated by Benjamin Whorf, an amateur linguist, and anthropologist Edward Sapir.[74] Following Sapir's theoretical work, Whorf found that the language spoken by the Hopi represents a view of reality that is dramatically different from more familiar tongues. For example, the Hopi language makes no distinction between nouns and verbs. Therefore, the people who speak it describe the entire world as being constantly in process. Whereas we use nouns to characterize people or objects as being fixed or constant, the Hopi view them more as verbs, constantly changing. In this sense our language represents much of the world rather like a snapshot camera, whereas Hopi reflects a worldview more like video.

Although the Sapir-Whorf hypothesis originally focused on foreign languages, Neil Postman illustrates the principle with an example closer to home. He describes a hypothetical culture where physicians identify patients they treat as "doing" arthritis and other diseases instead of "having" them and where criminals are diagnosed as "having" cases of criminality instead of "being" criminals.[75]

The implications of such a linguistic difference are profound. We believe that characteristics people "have"—what they "are"—are beyond their control, whereas they are responsible for what they "do." If we changed our view of what people "have" and what they "do," our attitudes would most likely change as well. Postman illustrates the consequences of this linguistic difference as applied to education:

In schools, for instance, we find that tests are given to determine how smart someone is or, more precisely, how much smartness someone "has." If one child scores a 138, and another a 106, the first is thought to "have" more smartness than the other. But this seems to me a strange conception—every bit as strange as "doing" arthritis or "having" criminality. I do not know anyone who *has* smartness. The people I know sometimes *do* smart things (as far as I can judge) and sometimes *do* stupid things—depending on what circumstances they are in, and how much they know about a situation, and how interested they are. "Smartness," so it seems to me, is a specific performance, done in a particular set of circumstances. It is not something you *are* or have in measurable quantities. . . . What I am driving at is this: All language is metaphorical, and often in the subtlest ways. In the simplest sentence, sometimes in the simplest word, we do more than merely express ourselves. We construct reality along certain lines. We make the world according to our own imagery.[76]

Subtle changes like this illustrate the theme of this chapter: that language is a powerful force for shaping our thoughts, and our relationship with others.

Summary

Language is both one of humanity's greatest assets and the source of many problems. This chapter highlighted the characteristics that distinguish language and suggested methods of using it more effectively.

Any language is a collection of symbols governed by a variety of rules and used to convey messages between people. Because of its symbolic nature, language is not a precise tool: Meanings rest in people, not in words themselves. In order for effective communication to occur, it is necessary to negotiate meanings for ambiguous statements.

Language not only describes people, ideas, processes, and events; it also shapes our perceptions of them in areas including status, credibility, and attitudes about gender and ethnicity. Along with influencing our attitudes, language reflects them. The words we use and our manner of speech reflect power, responsibility, affiliation, attraction, and interest.

Many types of language have the potential to create misunderstandings. Other types of language can result in unnecessary conflicts. In other cases, speech and writing can be evasive, avoiding expression of unwelcome messages.

The relationship between gender and language is complex. There are many differences in the ways men and women speak: The content of their conversations varies, as do their reasons for communicating and their conversational styles. Not all differences in language use can be accounted for by the speaker's gender, however. Occupation, social philosophy, and orientation toward problem solving also influence the use of language, and psychological sex role can be more of an influence than biological sex.

Language operates on a broad level to shape the consciousness and communication of an entire society. Different languages often shape and reflect the views of a culture. Low-context cultures like that of the United States use language primarily to express feelings and ideas as clearly and unambiguously as possible, whereas high-context cultures avoid specificity to promote social harmony. Some cultures value brevity and the succinct use of language, whereas others value elaborate forms of speech. In some societies formality is important, whereas in others informality is important. Beyond these differences, there is evidence to support linguistic relativism—the notion that language exerts a strong influence on the worldview of the people who speak it.

Key Terms

abstract language 82
abstraction ladder 82
behavioral description 83
convergence 77
divergence 78
emotive language 85
equivocal words 79
equivocation 87
euphemism 86
factual statement 84
high-context culture 93
inferential statement 85
jargon 81
language 68

linguistic relativism 96
low-context culture 93
opinion statement 84
phonological rules 70
pragmatic rules 71
relative words 80
Sapir-Whorf hypothesis 97
semantic rules 71
sex role 91
slang 81
symbols 68
syntactic rules 70

Activities

1. **Powerful Speech and Polite Speech** Increase your ability to achieve an optimal balance between powerful speech and polite speech by rehearsing one of the following scenarios:

   - Describing your qualifications to a potential employer for a job that interests you.

   - Requesting an extension on a deadline from one of your professors.

   - Explaining to a merchant why you want a cash refund on an unsatisfactory piece of merchandise when the store's policy is to issue credit vouchers.

   - Asking your boss for three days off so you can attend a friend's out-of-town wedding.

   - Approaching your neighbors whose dog barks while they are away from home.

   Your statement should gain its power by avoiding the types of powerless language listed in Table 3-1. You should not become abusive or threatening, and your statement should be completely honest.

2. **Slang and Jargon** Find a classmate, neighbor, coworker, or other person whose background differs significantly from yours. In an interview, ask this person to identify the slang and jargon terms that you take for granted but that he or she has found confusing. Explore the following types of potentially confusing terms:

   1. regionalisms
   2. age-related terms
   3. technical jargon
   4. acronyms

3. **Low-Level Abstractions** You can develop your ability to use low-level abstractions by following these steps:

   1. Use your own experience to write each of the following:
      a. a complaint or gripe
      b. one way you would like someone with whom you interact to change
      c. one reason why you appreciate a person with whom you interact

   2. Now translate each of the statements you have written into a low-level abstraction by including:
      a. the person or people involved
      b. the circumstances in which the behavior occurs
      c. the specific behaviors to which you are referring

   3. Compare the statements you have written in Steps 1 and 2. How might the lower-level abstractions in Step 2 improve the chances of having your message understood and accepted?

4. **Gender and Language**

   1. Note differences in the language use of three men and three women you know. Include yourself in the analysis. Your analysis will be most accurate if you tape record the speech of each person you analyze. Consider the following categories:

      conversational content   conversational style
      reasons for communicating   use of powerful/powerless speech

   2. Based on your observations, answer the following questions:
      a. How much does gender influence speech?
      b. What role do other variables play? Consider occupational or social status, cultural background, social philosophy, competitive-cooperative orientation, and other factors in your analysis.

For Further Exploration

For more resources about language, see the *Understanding Human Communication* website at www.oup.com/us/uhc10. There you will find a variety of resources: a list of books and articles, links to descriptions of feature films and television shows at the *Now Playing* website, study aids, and a self-test to check your understanding of the material in this chapter.

CHAPTER HIGHLIGHTS

We are attracted to other people for a variety of reasons: appearance, similarity, complementarity, their interest in us, competence, disclosure, proximity, and rewards.

Truly interpersonal communication has several characteristics that make it worth studying:

- It is qualitatively different from less personal relationships.
- Like all messages, qualitatively interpersonal communication has both content and relational dimensions.
- Interpersonal communication can address relational matters explicitly through metacommunication.

Communication scholars have explored some forces that shape interpersonal relationships:

- Developmental models describe how communication in relationships changes over time.
- Dialectical models describe forces that always operate in relationships.
- No matter which model is used to describe them, relationships are constantly changing.

Intimacy is a special dimension of interpersonal relationships:

- It has several dimensions.
- Men and women sometimes value and express intimacy differently.
- Cultural background influences how we communicate intimacy.

The subject of self-disclosure is an important one in the study of interpersonal relationships:

- People disclose (or withhold) personal information for a variety of reasons.
- Models can help us understand how self-disclosure operates.
- Regardless its purpose, self-disclosure in relationships possesses several characteristics.
- Several guidelines can help you decide whether or not to disclose personal information.

CHAPTER 6

Understanding Interpersonal Relationships

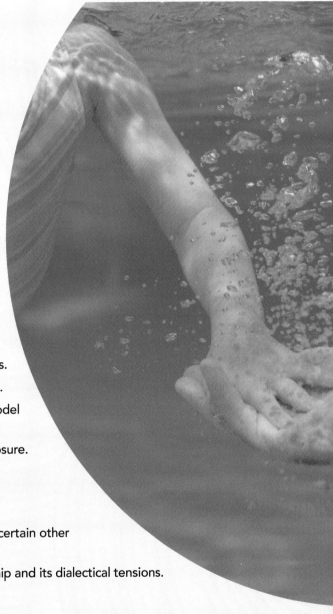

After studying the material in this chapter . . .

You should understand:

1. The factors that shape interpersonal attraction.
2. Knapp's model of relational development.
3. Dialectical tensions in interpersonal relationships.
4. The characteristics that distinguish interpersonal relationships from impersonal ones.
5. The content and relational dimensions of messages.
6. The role of metacommunication in relational messages.
7. Dimensions and influences of intimacy in relationships.
8. Reasons for self-disclosure and the Johari Window model of self-disclosure.
9. Characteristics of effective and appropriate self-disclosure.
10. The functions served by lies, equivocation, and hints.

You should be able to:

1. Describe the factors that cause you to be attracted to certain other individuals.
2. Identify the developmental stages of a given relationship and its dialectical tensions.
3. Identify interpersonal and impersonal communication.
4. Identify the content and relational dimensions of a message.
5. Distinguish among types of intimacy and influences on intimacy.
6. Identify the degree of self-disclosure in your relationships and the functions this serves.
7. Compose effective and appropriate disclosing messages.
8. Identify the types, functions, and ethical validity of nondisclosing messages you use.

Your own experience will show that some interpersonal relationships can be a source of tremendous satisfaction. Unfortunately, you probably know that other relationships can cause great pain. In this chapter we'll take a first look at the vitally important topic of interpersonal relationships. We will begin by exploring the reasons we form relationships with others. We will go on to explore two approaches that characterize how communication operates throughout the lifetime of relationships. Next, we'll explore what kinds of communication make some relationships much more personal than others. We will also look at some ways—both subtle and obvious—that we show others how we regard them and what kind of relationship we are seeking with them. Finally, we will look at the role of self-disclosure in interpersonal communication.

Why We Form Relationships

Sometimes we don't have a choice about our relationships: Children can't select their parents, and most workers aren't able to choose their bosses or colleagues. In many other cases, though, we seek out some people and actively avoid others. Social scientists have collected an impressive body of research on interpersonal attraction.[1] The following are some of the factors they have identified that influence our choice of relational partners.

Appearance

Most people claim that we should judge others on the basis of character, not appearance. The reality, however, is quite the opposite—at least in the early stages of a relationship.[2] In one study, a group of over 700 men and women were matched as blind dates, allegedly for a "computer dance." After the party was over, they were asked whether or not they would like to date their partners again. The result? The more physically attractive the person (as judged in advance by independent raters), the more likely he or she was seen as desirable. Other factors—social skills and intelligence, for example—didn't seem to affect the decision.[3]

Even if your appearance isn't beautiful by societal standards, consider these encouraging facts: First, after initial impressions have passed, ordinary-looking people with pleasing personalities are likely to be judged as attractive.[4] Second, physical factors become less important as a relationship progresses.[5] As one social scientist put it, "Attractive features may open doors, but apparently, it takes more than physical beauty to keep them open."[6]

Similarity

A large body of research confirms the fact that, in most cases, we like people who are similar to us.[7] For example, the more similar a married couple's personalities are, the more likely they are to report being happy and satisfied in their marriage.[8] Friends in middle and high school report being similar to one another in many ways, including having mutual friends, enjoying the same sports, liking the same social activities, and using (or not using) alcohol and cigarettes to the same degree.[9] For adults, similarity is more important to relational happiness than even communication ability: Friends who

"That's a good look for you, J.B."

have equally low levels of communication skills are just as satisfied with their relationships as are friends having high levels of communication skills.[10]

Attraction is greatest when we are similar to others in a high percentage of important areas. For example, two people who support each other's career goals, enjoy the same friends, and have similar beliefs about human rights can tolerate trivial disagreements about the merits of sushi or hip-hop music.

Complementarity

The folk wisdom that "opposites attract" seems to contradict the similarity principle just described. In truth, both are valid. Differences strengthen a relationship when they are *complementary*—when each partner's characteristics satisfy the other's needs. Individuals, for instance, are often likely to be attracted to each other when one partner is dominant and the other passive.[11] Relationships also work well when the partners agree that one will exercise control in certain areas ("You make the final decisions about money") and the other will exercise control in different areas ("I'll decide how we ought to decorate the place"). Strains occur when control issues are disputed.

When successful and unsuccessful couples are compared over a twenty-year period, it becomes clear that partners in successful marriages are similar enough to satisfy each other physically and mentally but different enough to meet each other's needs and keep the relationship interesting. Successful couples find ways to keep a balance between their similarities and differences, adjusting to the changes that occur over the years. We'll have more to say about balancing similarities and differences later in this chapter.

Reciprocal Attraction

We are attracted to people who like us—usually.[12] The power of reciprocal attraction is especially strong in the early stages of a relationship. Conversely, we will probably not care for people who either attack or seem indifferent toward us.

It's no mystery why reciprocal liking builds attractiveness. People who approve of us bolster our feelings of self-esteem. This approval is rewarding in its own right, and it can also confirm a presenting self-concept that says, "I'm a likable person."

Of course, we aren't drawn toward everyone who seems to like us. If we don't find the other person's attributes attractive, their interest can be a turn-off. Attraction has to be mutual if relationships are to succeed.

Competence

We like to be around talented people, probably because we hope their skills and abilities will rub off on us. On the other hand, we are uncomfortable around those who are *too* competent—probably because we look bad by comparison. Given these contrasting attitudes, it's no surprise that people are generally attracted to those who are talented but who have visible flaws that show that they are human, just like us.[13]

There are some qualifications to this principle. People with especially high or low self-esteem find "perfect" people more attractive than those who are competent but flawed, and some studies suggest that women tend to be more impressed by uniformly superior people of both sexes, whereas men tend to be more impressed by desirable but "human" subjects. On the whole, though, the principle stands: The best way to gain the liking of others is to be good at what you do but to admit your mistakes.

Disclosure

Revealing important information about yourself can help build liking.[14] Sometimes the basis of this liking comes from learning about how we are similar, either in experiences ("I broke off an engagement myself") or in attitudes ("I feel nervous with strangers, too"). Self-disclosure also builds liking because it is a sign of regard. When people share private information with you, it suggests that they respect and trust you—a kind of liking that we've already seen increases attractiveness. Disclosure plays an even more important role as relationships develop beyond their earliest stages.

Not all disclosure leads to liking. The information you reveal ought to be appropriate for the setting and stage of the relationship. You'll read more about self-disclosure later in this chapter.

Proximity

In many cases, proximity leads to liking.[15] For instance, we're more likely to develop friendships with close neighbors than with distant ones, and chances are good that we'll choose a mate with whom we cross paths often. Facts like these are understandable when we consider that proximity allows us to get more information about other people and benefit from a relationship with them. Also, people in close proximity may be more similar to us than those not close—for example, if we live in the same neighborhood, odds are we share the same socioeconomic status. The Internet provides a new means for creating closeness, as users are able to experience "virtual proximity" in cyberspace.[16]

Familiarity, on the other hand, can also breed contempt. Thieves frequently prey on nearby victims, even though the risk of being recognized is greater. Spousal and child abuse are distressingly common. Most aggravated assaults occur within the family or among close neighbors. With regard to crimes, the same principle holds: You are likely to develop strong personal feelings of either like or dislike regarding others you encounter frequently.

"I'd like to buy everyone a drink. All I ask in return is that you listen patiently to my shallow and simplistic views on a broad range of social and political issues."
Source: © Cartoonbank.com

Rewards

Some social scientists argue that all relationships—both impersonal and personal—are based on a semi-economic model called *social exchange theory*.[17] This model suggests that we often seek out people who can give us rewards that are greater than or equal to the costs we encounter in dealing with them. Rewards may be tangible (a nice place to live, a high-paying job) or intangible (prestige, emotional support, companionship). Costs are undesirable outcomes: unpleasant work, emotional pain, and so on. A simple formula captures the social exchange theory of why we form and maintain relationships:

$$Rewards - Costs = Outcome$$

According to social exchange theorists, we use this formula (usually unconsciously) to decide whether dealing with another person is a "good deal" or "not worth the effort," based on whether the outcome is positive or negative.

At its most blatant level, an exchange approach seems cold and calculating, but in some types of relationships it seems quite appropriate. A healthy business relationship is based on how well the parties help one another, and some friendships are based on an informal kind of barter: "I don't mind listening to the ups and downs of your love life because you rescue me when the house needs repairs." Even close relationships have an element of exchange. Friends and lovers often tolerate each other's quirks because the comfort and enjoyment they get make the less-than-pleasant times worth accepting. In more serious cases, social exchange explains why some people stay in abusive relationships. Sadly, these people often report that they would rather be in a bad relationship than have no relationship at all.

Characteristics of Interpersonal Communication

What is interpersonal communication? How does it differ from other types of interaction? When and how are interpersonal messages communicated? Read on and see.

What Makes Communication Interpersonal?

The most obvious way to define *interpersonal communication* is by looking at the number of people involved. In this sense we could say that all communication between two people, or **contextually interpersonal communication,** is interpersonal.

In many ways, contextually interpersonal communication *is* different from the kind that goes on in other contexts, such as the kinds of small groups discussed in Chapters 8 and 9 of this book. For example, unlike threesomes and other groups, dyads are complete and cannot be subdivided. If one person withdraws from the other, the relationship is finished. This indivisibility means that, unlike groups, the partners in a dyad can't form coalitions to get their needs met: They must work matters out with one another. Likewise, dyadic communication differs from the kinds of public speeches described in Chapters 10–14 and from most types of mass communication.

Although looking at communication by context is useful, this approach raises some problems. Consider, for example, a routine transaction between a sales clerk and customer, or the rushed exchange when you ask a stranger on the street for directions. Communication of this sort hardly seems interpersonal—or personal in any sense of the word. In fact, after transactions like this we commonly remark, "I might as well have been talking to a machine."

The impersonal nature of some two-person exchanges has led some scholars to say that quality, not quantity, is what distinguishes interpersonal communication. **Qualitatively interpersonal communication** occurs when people treat one another as unique individuals, regardless of the context in which the interaction occurs or the number of people involved.[18]

When quality of interaction is the criterion, the opposite of interpersonal communication is *impersonal* interaction, not group, public, or mass communication.

The majority of our communication, even in dyadic contexts, is relatively impersonal. We chat pleasantly with shopkeepers or fellow passengers on the bus or plane; we discuss the weather or current events with most classmates and neighbors; we deal with coworkers in a polite way. Considering the number of people we communicate with, qualitatively interpersonal interaction is rather scarce. This scarcity isn't necessarily unfortunate: Most of us don't have the time or energy to create personal relationships with everyone we encounter—or even to act in a personal way all the time with the people we know and love best. In fact, the scarcity of qualitatively interpersonal communication contributes to its value. Like precious jewels and one-of-a-kind artwork, qualitatively interpersonal relationships are special because of their scarcity. You can get a sense of how interpersonal your relationships are by trying Activity number 1 at the end of the chapter.

Interpersonal Communication and the Internet

There's no question that mediated relationships conducted via e-mail, instant messaging, and telephone pass the test of being contextually interpersonal. But what about their quality? Is online communication a poor substitute for face-to-face contact, or is it a rich medium for developing close personal relationships? As the reading on page 169 shows, either can be true.

In one survey, approximately 25 percent of the respondents who used the Internet regularly reported spending less time talking in person and on the phone with friends and family members.[19] Another survey revealed that people who relied heavily on the Internet to meet their communication needs grew to rely less and less on their face-to-face networks. More significantly, they tended to feel more lonely and depressed as their online communication increased.[20]

Despite findings like these, a growing body of research disputes the notion that mediated communication lacks quality.[21] Writing (online, of course) in *CMC Magazine*, Brittney G. Chenault summarized research concluding that e-mail, chat rooms, Internet newsgroups, and computer conferences can and do allow electronic correspondents to develop a degree of closeness similar to what can be achieved in person.[22]

Research confirms the claim that mediated communication can *enhance*, not diminish, the quantity and quality of interpersonal communication. Over half of the respondents in one survey reported that the number of their personal relationships had grown since they started to use the Internet. In another survey of over 3,000 adults in the United States (again, both Internet users and nonusers), 72 percent of the Internet users had communicated with a relative or a friend within the past day, compared with 61 percent for nonusers.[23] Surprisingly, the Internet users were also more likely to have phoned friends and relatives.

Even more significant than the amount of communication that occurs online is its quality: 55 percent of Internet users said that e-mail had improved communications with family, and 66 percent said that their contact with friends had increased because of e-mail. Among women, the rate of satisfaction was even higher: 60 percent reported better contact with family and 71 percent with friends. Over three-quarters of the Internet users polled said they never felt ignored by another household member's spending time online.[24] The majority of the Internet users said that e-mail, websites, and chat rooms had a "modestly positive impact" on their ability to communicate more with family members and make new friends. Among women, the rate of satisfaction

UNDERSTANDING COMMUNICATION TECHNOLOGY
What Am I, Chopped Spam?

I'm coming to terms with my need for spam filters against my friends' e-mail.

I'm glad to see a joke or an article that they picked out for me, but not one that they blasted to everyone in their address book. Did they really imagine I wanted to drop everything this second to contemplate the future of NATO? Are they writing personal notes to their A-list friends and relegating me to the @-list? What am I, chopped Spam?

What we have here is obviously not a failure to communicate, but it's not quite the opposite either. It's not a simple case of information overload, according to a seminar by Dr. [Dan] Ryan, a professor at Mills College in Oakland, Calif.

Every message incorporates another message in the way it is delivered, whether it's an e-mail or a ransom note pinned to an ear. Dr. Ryan said that in barraging me with "friendly-fire spam," my correspondents were also telling me: "I'm too busy to be bothered thinking much about whether and why you, recipient, might actually want to know this. At this moment I'm treating you just like everyone else in my address book."

Yes, those messages came through pretty clearly, although I like to think my friends didn't mean to do all that metanotify-ing. They presumably figured I might be interested in what they were thinking—and often I am.

But it's still spam, and you don't expect that from friends. It's the equivalent of the holiday cards with the what-our-family-did-last-year letter. We recognize that these letters serve a purpose—and we realize that the writers don't have time to send personal letters to all their friends. But the mass-produced pseudo-intimacy still seems dorky.

That's why, as Dr. Ryan pointed out, so many of these holiday dispatches begin with an apology like, "We hate these photocopied letters, too." The most diligent will scribble a brief personal note on the letter to send a further message: See, you're not like all the others. We have a relationship!

That's the kind of signal I've started looking for in the e-mail messages from my friends-turned-spammers—some recognition that I'm more than just a Contact. I'm trying filters that distinguish letters with a small display of netiquette, like having my name somewhere besides the address line. I'm not looking for a long personal note. It's the metanotification that counts.

Excerpted from John Tierney, "As the Grapevine Withers, Spam Filters Take Root."

---

was even higher: 60 percent reported better contact with family and 61 percent with friends.

For some people, the lack of immediacy in online communication makes it easier to build close relationships. Sociolinguist Deborah Tannen describes a situation where e-mail enhanced a relationship that wouldn't have developed to the same degree in person:

> E-mail deepened my friendship with Ralph. Though his office was next to mine, we rarely had extended conversations because he is shy. Face to face he mumbled so I could barely tell he was speaking. But when we both got on e-mail, I started receiving long, self-revealing messages; we poured our hearts out to each other. A friend discovered that e-mail opened up that kind of communication with her father. He would never talk much on the phone (as her mother would), but they have become close since they both got on line.[25]

Stories like these suggest that, rather than weakening opportunities for communication, CMC provides rich opportunities for establishing and maintaining relationships. An Internet connection makes it possible to send and receive messages at any time of the day or night from people around the world. In cases where face-to-face contact is impossible and telephone conversations difficult due to cost or time differences, computer-mediated messages are cheap, quick, and easy.

CULTURAL IDIOM

Poured our hearts out:
revealed our innermost thoughts and feelings

Content and Relational Messages

Virtually every verbal statement contains two kinds of messages. **Content messages,** which focus on the subject being discussed, are the most obvious. The content of such statements as "It's your turn to do the dishes" or "I'm busy Saturday night" is obvious.

Content messages aren't the only kind that are exchanged when two people interact. In addition, virtually all communication—both verbal and nonverbal—contains **relational messages,** which make statements about how the parties feel toward one another.[26] These relational messages express communicators' feelings and attitudes involving one or more dimensions:

Affinity   One dimension of relational communication is **affinity:** the degree to which people like or appreciate one another.

Respect   **Respect** is the degree to which we admire others and hold them in esteem. Respect and affinity might seem identical, but they are actually different dimensions of a relationship.[27] For example, you might like a three-year-old child tremendously without respecting her. Likewise, you could respect a boss or teacher's talents without liking him or her. Respect is a tremendously important and often overlooked ingredient in satisfying relationships. It is a better predictor of relational satisfaction than liking, or even loving.[28]

Immediacy   Communication scholars use the term **immediacy** to describe the degree of interest and attraction we feel toward and communicate to others. Immediacy is different than affinity. You can like someone (high affinity) but not demonstrate that feeling (low immediacy). Likewise, it's easy to imagine high affinity/high immediacy and low affinity/low immediacy, as well as low affinity and high immediacy. Which of these conditions do you think exists in the photo on this page?

Control   In every conversation and every relationship there is some distribution of **control:** the amount of influence communicators seek. Control can be distributed evenly among relational partners, or one person can have more and the other(s) less. An uneven distribution of control won't cause problems as long as everyone involved accepts that arrangement. Struggles arise, though, when people disagree on how control should be distributed in their relationship.

You can get a feeling for how relational messages operate in everyday life by recalling the statements at the beginning of this section. Imagine two ways of saying "It's your turn to do the dishes": one that is demanding and another that is matter-of-fact. Notice how the different nonverbal messages make statements about how the sender views control in this part of the relationship. The demanding tone says, in effect, "I have a right to tell you what to do around the house," whereas the matter-of-fact one suggests, "I'm just reminding you of something you might have overlooked." Likewise, you can easily visualize two ways to deliver the statement "I'm busy Saturday night": one with little affection and the other with much liking.

Notice that in each of these examples the relational dimension of the message was never discussed. In fact, most of the time we aren't conscious of the relational messages that bombard us every day. Sometimes we are unaware of relational messages because they match our belief about the amount of respect, immediacy, control, and affinity that is appropriate. For example, you probably won't be offended if your boss tells you to do a certain job, because you agree that supervisors have the right to direct employees. In other cases, however, conflicts arise over relational messages even though content is not disputed. If your boss delivers the order in a condescending, sarcastic, or abusive tone of voice, you probably will be offended. Your complaint wouldn't be with the order itself but rather with the way it was delivered. "I may work for this company," you might think, "but I'm not a slave or an idiot. I deserve to be treated like a human being."

How are relational messages communicated? As the boss-employee example suggests, they are usually expressed nonverbally. To test this fact for yourself, imagine how you could act while saying "Can you help me for a minute?" in a way that communicates each of the following attitudes:

CULTURAL IDIOM

On the one hand:
from one point of view

superiority	aloofness	friendliness
helplessness	sexual desire	irritation

Although nonverbal behaviors are a good source of relational messages, remember that they are ambiguous. The sharp tone you take as a personal insult might be due to fatigue, and the interruption you take as an attempt to ignore your ideas might be a sign of pressure that has nothing to do with you. Before you jump to conclusions about relational clues, it's a good idea to practice the skill of perception checking that you learned in Chapter 2: "When you use that tone of voice to tell me it's my turn to do the dishes, I get the idea you're mad at me. Is that right?" If your interpretation was indeed correct, you can talk about the problem. On the other hand, if you were overreacting, the perception check can prevent a needless fight.

Metacommunication

As the preceding example of perception checking shows, not all relational messages are nonverbal. Social scientists use the term **metacommunication** to describe messages that refer to other messages.[29] In other words, metacommunication is communication about communication. Whenever we discuss a relationship with others, we are metacommunicating: "It sounds like you're angry at me" or "I appreciate how honest you've been." As the cartoon on this page shows, even text messages can contain metacommunicative dimensions. An e-mail or instant message that calls you an "idiot" might be a joking token of affection, or something quite the opposite. Given the fact that nonverbal cues are limited in computer-mediated communication, it's often important to supplement them with metacommunication (such as "just kidding").

Metacommunication is an important method of solving conflicts in a constructive manner. It provides a way to shift discussion from the content level to relational questions, where the problem often lies. For example, consider a couple bickering because one partner wants to watch television, whereas the other wants to talk. Imagine how much better the chances of a positive outcome would be if they used metacommunication to examine the relational problems that were behind their quarrel: "Look, it's not the TV watching itself that bothers me. It's that I imagine you watch so much because you're mad at me or bored. Are you feeling bad about us?"

Metacommunication isn't just a tool for handling problems. It is also a way to reinforce the good aspects of a relationship: "I really appreciate it when you compliment me about my work in front of the boss." Comments like this serve two functions: First, they let others know that you value their behavior. Second, they boost the odds that the other people will continue the behavior in the future.

Despite the benefits of metacommunication, bringing relational issues out in the open does have its risks. Discussing problems can be interpreted in two ways. On the one hand, the other person might see it in a positive

"She's texting me, but I think she's also subtexting me."
Source: © Cartoonbank.com

CULTURAL IDIOM

On the other hand:
from the other point of view

light—"Our relationship is working because we can still talk things out." On the other hand, your desire to focus on the relationship might look like a bad omen—"Our relationship isn't working if we have to keep talking it over." Furthermore, metacommunication does involve a certain degree of analysis ("It seems like you're angry at me"), and some people resent being analyzed. These cautions don't mean verbal metacommunication is a bad idea. They do suggest, though, that it's a tool that needs to be used carefully.

Communication over the Relational Life Span

Qualitatively interpersonal relationships aren't stable. Instead, they are constantly changing. Communication scholars have described the way relationships develop and shift in two ways. We will examine each of them now.

A Developmental Perspective

One of the best-known explanations of how communication operates in relationships was created by Mark Knapp, whose **developmental model** broke down the rise and fall of relationships into ten stages, contained in the two broad phases of "coming together" and "coming apart."[30] Other researchers have suggested that any model of relational communication ought to contain a third part of relational maintenance—communication aimed at keeping relationships operating smoothly and satisfactorily.[31] Figure 6-1 shows how Knapp's ten stages fit into this three-part view of relational communication.

The following stages are especially descriptive of intimate, romantic relationships and close friendships. The pattern for other intimate relationships, such as families, would follow different paths.

Initiating   The stage of initiation involves the initial making of contact with another person. Knapp restricts this stage to conversation openers, both in initial contacts and in contacts with acquaintances: "Nice to meet you," "How's it going?" and so on.

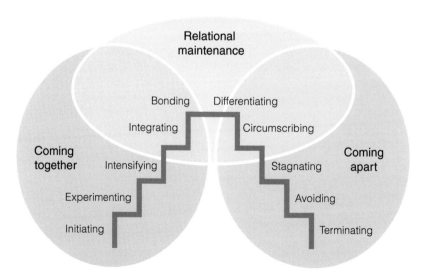

FIGURE 6-1   Stages of Relational Development

Whatever your preference for opening remarks, this stage is important because you are formulating your first impressions and presenting yourself as interested in the other person.

Initiating relationships can be particularly hard for people who are shy. Making contact via the Internet can be helpful for people who have a hard time conversing in person. One study of an online dating service found that participants who identified themselves as shy expressed a greater appreciation for the system's anonymous, nonthreatening environment than did nonshy users.[32] The researchers found that many shy users employed the online service specifically to help overcome their inhibitions about initiating relationships in face-to-face settings.

CULTURAL IDIOM
"small talk":
unimportant or trivial conversation

Experimenting In the stage of experimenting, conversation develops as people get acquainted by making "small talk." We ask: "Where are you from?" or "What do you do?" or "Do you know Josephine Mandoza? She lives in San Francisco, too."

Though small talk might seem meaningless, Knapp points out that it serves four purposes:

- It is a useful process for uncovering integrating topics and openings for more penetrating conversation.
- It can be an audition for a future friendship or a way of increasing the scope of a current relationship.
- It provides a safe procedure for indicating who we are and how another can come to know us better (reduction of uncertainty).
- It allows us to maintain a sense of community with our fellow human beings.

The relationship during this stage is generally pleasant and uncritical, and the commitments are minimal. Experimenting may last ten minutes or ten years, and it can happen online as well as in person. One study revealed that three out of four Internet users who are looking for a romantic partner have tried at least once to reach out online.

Intensifying At the next stage, the kind of truly interpersonal relationship defined earlier in this chapter begins to develop. Several changes in communication patterns occur during intensifying. The expression of feelings toward the other becomes more common. Dating couples use a wide range of communication strategies to describe their feelings of attraction.[33] About a quarter of the time they express their feelings directly, using metacommunication to discuss the state of the relationship. More often they use less-direct methods of communication: spending an increasing amount of time together, asking for support from one another, doing favors for the partner, giving tokens of affection, hinting and flirting, expressing feelings nonverbally, getting to know the partner's friends and family, and trying to look more physically attractive. Touching is more common during this stage than in either earlier or later ones.[34] Other changes mark the intensifying stage. Forms of address become more familiar. The parties begin to see themselves as "we" instead of as separate individuals. It is during the intensifying stage that individuals begin to directly express feelings of commitment to one another: "I'm sure glad we met." "You're the best thing that's happened to me in a long time."

Integrating As the relationship strengthens, the parties begin to take on an identity as a social unit. Invitations begin to come addressed to the couple. Social circles merge. The partners begin to take on each other's commitments: "Sure, we'll spend Thanksgiving with your family." Common property may begin to be designated—our apartment, our car, our song.[35] Partners develop their own rituals for everything from expressing intimacy to handling daily routines.[36] They even begin to speak alike, using common words and sentence patterns.[37] In this sense, the integration stage is a time when we give up some characteristics of our old selves and become different people.

As we become more integrated with others, our sense of obligation to them grows.[38] We feel obliged to provide a variety of resources such as class notes and money, whether or not the other person asks for them. When intimates do make requests of one another, they are relatively straightforward. Gone are the elaborate explanations, inducements, and apologies. In short, partners in an integrated relationship expect more from one another than they do in less-intimate associations.

Bonding   During the bonding stage, the parties make symbolic public gestures to show the world that their relationship exists. The most common form of bonding in romantic relationships is a wedding ceremony and the legal ties that come with it. Bonding generates social support for the relationship. Both custom and law impose certain obligations on partners who have officially bonded.

Bonding marks a turning point in a relationship. Up to now the relationship may have developed at a steady pace: Experimenting gradually moved into intensifying and then into integrating. Now, however, there is a spurt of commitment. The public display and declaration of exclusivity make this a critical period in the relationship.

Relationships don't have to be romantic to have a bonding stage. Business contracts form a bond, as does being initiated into a fraternity or sorority. Acts like these "officialize" a relationship and involve a measure of public commitment.

Differentiating   Now that the two people have formed this commonalty, they need to reestablish individual identities. This is the point where the "hold me tight" orientation that has existed shifts, and "put me down" messages begin to occur. Partners use a variety of strategies to gain privacy from one another.[39] Sometimes they confront the other party directly, explaining that they don't want to continue a discussion. At other times they are less direct, offering nonverbal cues, changing the topic, or leaving the room.

Differentiation is likely to occur when a relationship begins to experience the first, inevitable stress. This need for autonomy needn't be a negative experience, however. People need to be individuals as well as parts of a relationship, and differentiation is a necessary step toward autonomy. As you'll read later in this chapter, the key to successful differentiation is maintaining a commitment to the relationship while creating the space for being an individual as well.

Circumscribing   In the circumscribing stage, communication between members decreases in quantity and quality. Restrictions and restraints characterize this stage, and dynamic communication becomes static. Rather than discuss a disagreement (which requires some degree of energy on both parts), members opt for withdrawal: either mental (silence or daydreaming and fantasizing) or physical (where people spend less time together). Circumscribing doesn't involve total avoidance, which comes later. Rather, it entails a certain shrinking of interest and commitment.

Stagnating   If circumscribing continues, the relationship begins to stagnate. Members behave toward each other in old, familiar ways without much feeling. No growth occurs. The relationship is a shadow of its former self. We see stagnation in many workers who have lost enthusiasm for their job yet continue to go through the motions for years. The same sad event occurs for some couples who unenthusiastically have the same conversations, see the same people, and follow the same routines without any sense of joy or novelty.

Avoiding   When stagnation becomes too unpleasant, parties in a relationship begin to create distance between each other. Sometimes this is done under the guise of excuses ("I've been sick lately and can't see you"), and sometimes it is done directly ("Please don't call me; I don't want to see you now"). In either case, by this point the handwriting about the relationship's future is clearly on the wall.

Terminating   Characteristics of this final stage include summary dialogues about where the relationship has gone and the desire to dissociate. The relationship may end with a cordial dinner, a note left on the kitchen table, a phone call, or a legal document stating the dissolution. Depending on each person's feelings, this stage can be quite short, or it may be drawn out over time, with bitter jabs at one another.

The deterioration of a relationship from bonding to circumscribing, stagnating, and avoiding isn't inevitable. One of the key differences between marriages that end in separation and those that are restored to their former intimacy is the communication that occurs when the partners are unsatisfied.[40] Unsuccessful couples deal with their problems by avoidance, indirectness, and less involvement with one another. By contrast, couples who "repair" their relationship communicate much more directly. They air their concerns and spend time and effort negotiating solutions to their problems.

Relationships don't always move toward termination in a straight line. Rather, they take a back-and-forth pattern, where the trend is toward dissolution.[41]

While the communication surrounding relational termination can sometimes be cruel and painful (see the reading on page 176), it doesn't have to be totally negative. Understanding each other's investment in the relationships and need for personal growth may dilute the hard feelings. In fact, many relationships aren't so much terminated as redefined. A divorced couple, for example, may find new, less intimate ways to relate to each other.

CULTURAL IDIOM

handwriting . . . is clearly on the wall:
an indication or foretelling of an unfortunate message

bitter jabs:
unkind comments

Knapp's model of relational development and decline offers a good description of communication stages in traditional romantic relationships. Some critics have argued that it doesn't characterize other sorts of relationships so well. Identify your position in this debate by following these steps:

1. Explain how well (or poorly) the model describes one other type of relationship: among coworkers, friends (either close or more distant), parent and child, or another relational context of your choosing.

2. Construct a model describing communication stages in the relationship type you just identified. How does this model differ from Knapp's?

CRITICAL THINKING PROBE

● **Stages in Nonromantic Relationships**

UNDERSTANDING COMMUNICATION TECHNOLOGY

To End a Romance, Just Press "Send": Instant Messaging Altering the Way We Love

It was the middle of a workday two weeks ago, and Larry was deep into a meeting when a text-message began scrolling across his cellphone screen. He glanced at it and thought: "You can't be serious."

It was no joke. His girlfriend was breaking up with him . . . again. And she was doing it by e-mail . . . again.

For the sixth time in eight months, she had ended their relationship electronically rather than face-to-face. He had sensed trouble—he had been opening his e-mail with trepidation for weeks—so the previous day he had suggested that they meet in person to talk things over. But she nixed that, instead choosing to send the latest in what Larry had begun to consider part of a virtual genre: "the goodbye e-mail."

Understandably, he'd like to say his own goodbye to that genre. "E-mail is horrible," says Larry, 36, an Air Force sergeant from New Hampshire who asked that his last name not be used. "You just get to the point where you hate it. You can't have dialogue. You don't have that person in front of you. You just have that black-and-white text. It's a very cold way of communicating."

Cold, maybe. Popular, for sure. The use of e-mail and instant-messaging to end intimate relationships is gaining popularity because instantaneous communication makes it easy—some say too easy—to just call the whole thing off. Want to avoid one of those squirmy, awkward breakup scenes? Want to control the dialogue while removing facial expressions, vocal inflections, and body language from the equation? A solution is as near as your keyboard or cellphone.

Sometimes there is a legitimate reason for wanting to avoid personal contact. Tara, a 32-year-old woman who lives near Boston, says her ex-husband was intimidating and emotionally abusive during their marriage.

So when she wanted to end the marriage several years ago, she felt more comfortable doing so by sending a text message.

Tara says that since then she has ended several other relationships by e-mail. "I'm a softie, and I hate hurting people's feelings," she says. Recently she laid the groundwork for breaking her engagement with a series of e-mails to her fiance. After ending the engagement last week, she reached a moment of truth, she says, and has decided that from now on, if she wants to call it quits, "The e-mail option is out."

This sort of back-and-forth might reflect what Lee Rainey, director of the Pew Internet & American Life Project, sees as a blurring of the boundaries in modern romance between the real and virtual realms.

"People are living, in many respects, with a foot in both worlds," Rainey says. "They've got virtual stuff sitting next to real-world stuff. But we haven't worked out the social norms yet. For some people, this will feel really callous. Others feel that, 'This is how I communicate these days, and why shouldn't I break up with someone by e-mail?' "

Don Aucoin, Globe Staff
Source: *The Boston Globe*, April 22, 2007, A1.

A Dialectical Perspective

Developmental models like the one described in the preceding pages suggest that communication differs in important ways at various points in the life of a relationship. According to these stage-related models, the kinds of interaction that happen during initiating, experimenting, or intensifying are different from the interaction that occurs during differentiating, circumscribing, or avoiding.

Not all theorists agree that a stage-related model is the best way to explain interaction in relationships. Some suggest that communicators grapple with the same kinds of challenges whether a relationship is brand-new or has lasted decades. They argue that communicators seek important but inherently incompatible goals throughout virtually all of their relationships. This **dialectical model** suggests that struggling to achieve these goals creates **dialectical tensions:** conflicts that arise when two opposing or incompatible forces exist simultaneously. In recent years, communication scholars have identified the dialectical tensions that make successful communication challenging.[42] They suggest that the struggle to manage these dialectical tensions creates the most powerful dynamics in relational communication. In the following pages we will discuss three powerful dialectical tensions.

Connection Versus Autonomy   No one is an island. Recognizing this fact, we seek out involvement with others. But, at the same time, we are unwilling to sacrifice our entire identity to even the most satisfying relationship. The conflicting desires for connection and independence are embodied in the *connection-autonomy dialectic*. Research on relational breakups demonstrates the consequences for relational partners who can't find a way to manage these very different personal needs.[43] Some of the most common reasons for relational breakups involve failure of partners to satisfy one another's needs for connection: "We barely spent any time together"; "He wasn't committed to the relationship"; "We had different needs." But other relational complaints involve excessive demands for connection: "I was feeling trapped"; "I needed freedom."

The levels of connection and autonomy that we seek can change over time. In his book *Intimate Behavior*, Desmond Morris suggests that each of us repeatedly goes through three stages: "Hold me tight," "Put me down," and "Leave me alone."[44] This cycle becomes apparent in the first years of life when children move from the "Hold me tight" stage that characterizes infancy into a new "Put me down" stage of exploring the world by crawling, walking, touching, and tasting. This move for independence isn't all in one direction: The same three-year-old who insists "I can do it myself" in August may cling to parents on the first day of preschool in September. As children grow into adolescents, the "Leave me alone" orientation becomes apparent. Teenagers who used to happily spend time with their parents now may groan at the thought of a family vacation or even the notion of sitting down at the dinner table each evening. More time is spent with friends or alone. Although this time can be painful for parents, most developmental experts recognize it as a necessary stage in moving from childhood to adulthood.

As the need for independence from family grows, adolescents take care of their "hold me tight" needs by associating with their peers. Friendships during the teenage years are vital, and the level of closeness with contemporaries can be a barometer of happiness. This is the time when physical intimacy becomes an option, and sexual exploration may provide a new way of achieving closeness.

In adult relationships, the same cycle of intimacy and distance repeats itself. In marriages, for example, the "Hold me tight" bonds of the first year are often followed by a desire for independence. This need for autonomy can manifest itself in a number of ways, such as the desire to make friends or engage in activities that don't include the spouse, or the need to make a career move that might disrupt the relationship. As the discussion of relational stages later in this chapter will explain, this movement from closeness to autonomy may lead to the breakup of relationships, but it can also be part of a cycle that redefines the relationship in a new form that can recapture or even surpass the intimacy that existed in the past.

Predictability Versus Novelty   Stability is an important need in relationships, but too much of it can lead to feelings of staleness. The *predictability-novelty dialectic* reflects this tension. Humorist Dave Barry exaggerates only slightly when he talks about the boredom that can come when husbands and wives know each other too well:

> After a decade or so of marriage, you know *everything* about your spouse, every habit and opinion and twitch and tic and minor skin growth. You could write a seventeen-pound book solely about the way your spouse *eats*. This kind of intimate knowledge can be very handy in certain situations—such as when you're on a TV quiz show where the object is to identify your spouse from the sound of his or her chewing—but it tends to lower the passion level of a relationship.[45]

Although too much familiarity can lead to the risk of boredom and stagnation, nobody wants a completely unpredictable relational partner. Too many surprises can

Source: Reprinted by special permission of King Features Syndicate.

threaten the foundations upon which the relationship is based ("You're not the person I married!").

The challenge for communicators is to juggle the desire for predictability with the need for novelty that keeps the relationship fresh and interesting. People differ in their need and desire for stability and surprises, so there is no optimal mixture of the two. As you will read shortly, there are a number of strategies people can use to manage these contradictory drives.

Openness Versus Privacy   As Chapter 1 explained, disclosure is one characteristic of interpersonal relationships. Yet, along with the need for intimacy, we have an equally important need to maintain some space between ourselves and others. These sometimes conflicting drives create the *openness-privacy dialectic.*

Even the strongest interpersonal relationships require some distance. On a short-term basis, the desire for closeness waxes and wanes. Lovers may go through periods of much sharing and times of relative withdrawal. Likewise, they experience periods of passion and then periods of little physical contact. Friends have times of high disclosure where they share almost every feeling and idea and then disengage for days, months, or even longer. Figure 6-2 illustrates some patterns of variation in openness uncovered in a study of college students' communication patterns.[46] The students reported the degree of openness in one of their important relationships—a friendship, romantic relationship, or marriage—over a range of 30 conversations. The graphs show a definite pattern of fluctuation between disclosure and privacy in every stage of the relationships.

Strategies for Managing Dialectical Tensions   Managing the dialectical tensions outlined in these pages presents communication challenges. There are a number of strategies by which these challenges can be managed.[47] One of the least functional is *denial* that tensions exist. People in denial insist that "everything is fine," that the inevitable tugs of dialectical tensions really aren't a problem. For example, coworkers who claim that they're *always* happy to be members of the team and *never* see conflicts between their personal goals and the organization's are probably operating in a state of denial.

Disorientation is another response to dialectical tensions. In this response, communicators feel so overwhelmed and helpless that they are unable to confront their problems. In the face of dialectical tensions they might fight, freeze, or even leave the relationship. A couple who discover soon after the honeymoon that living a "hap-

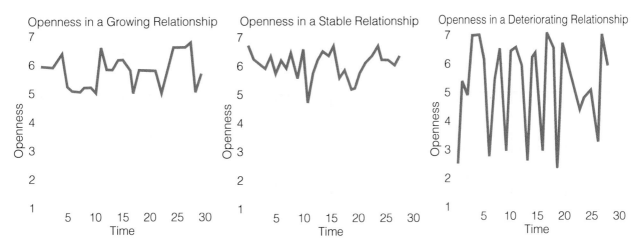

FIGURE 6-2 Cyclical Phases of Openness and Withdrawal in Relationships

pily ever after" conflict-free life is impossible might become so terrified that they would come to view their marriage as a mistake.

In the strategy of *selection*, communicators respond to one end of the dialectical spectrum and ignore the other. For example, a couple caught between the conflicting desires for stability and novelty might find their struggle to change too difficult to manage and choose to stick with predictable, if unexciting, patterns of relating to one another.

Communicators choose the strategy of *alternation* to alternate between one end of the dialectical spectrum at some times and the other end at other times. Friends, for example, might manage the autonomy-connection dialectic by alternating between times when they spend a large amount of time together and other times when they live independent lives.

A fifth strategy is *segmentation*, a tactic in which partners compartmentalize different areas of their relationship. For example, a couple might manage the openness-closedness dialectic by sharing almost all their feelings about mutual friends with one another but keeping certain parts of their past romantic histories private.

Moderation is a sixth strategy. This strategy is characterized by compromises, in which communicators choose to back off from expressing either end of the dialectical spectrum. Adult children, for example, might manage the revelation-concealment dialectic with their inquisitive parents by answering some (though not all) unwelcome parental questions.

Communicators can also respond to dialectical challenges by *reframing* them in terms that redefine the situation so that the apparent contradiction disappears. Consider a couple who wince when their friends characterize them as a "perfect couple." On one hand, they want to escape from the "perfect couple" label that feels confining, but on the other hand, they enjoy the admiration that comes with this identity. By pointing out to their friends that "ideal couples" aren't always blissfully happy, they can both be themselves and keep the admiration of their friends.

A final strategy for handling dialectical tensions is *reaffirmation*—acknowledging that dialectical tensions will never disappear, accepting or even embracing the challenges they present. The metaphorical view of relational life as a kind of roller coaster reflects this orientation, and communicators who use reaffirmation view dialectical tensions as part of the ride.

Even though a relationship may move back to a stage it has experienced before, it will never be the same. For example, most healthy long-term relationships will go through several phases of experimenting, when the partners try out new ways of behaving with one another. Though each phase is characterized by the same general features, the specifics will feel different each time. As you learned in Chapter 1, communication is irreversible. Partners can never go back to "the way things were." Sometimes this fact may lead to regrets: It's impossible to take back a cruel comment or forget a crisis. On the other hand, the irreversibility of communication can make relationships exciting, because it lessens the chance for boredom.

Intimacy in Interpersonal Relationships

Even the closest relationships involve a mixture of personal and interpersonal communication. We alternate between a "we" and a "me" orientation, sometimes focusing on connecting with others and at other times focusing on our own needs and interests. In the next few pages we will examine how our communication is affected by these apparently conflicting drives for intimacy and distance.

Dimensions of Intimacy

The dictionary defines *intimacy* as arising from "close union, contact, association, or acquaintance." This definition suggests that the key element of intimacy is closeness, one element that "ordinary people" have reported as characterizing their intimate relationships.[48] However, it doesn't explain what *kinds* of closeness can create a state of intimacy. In truth, **intimacy** can have several qualities. The first is *physical*. Even before birth, the developing fetus experiences a kind of physical closeness with its mother that will never happen again, "floating in a warm fluid, curling inside a total embrace, swaying to the undulations of the moving body and hearing the beat of the pulsing heart."[49] As they grow up, fortunate children are continually nourished by physical intimacy: being rocked, fed, hugged, and held. As we grow older, the opportunities for physical intimacy are less regular, but still possible and important. Some, but by no means all, physical intimacy is sexual. In one survey, only one-quarter of the respondents (who were college students) stated that intimacy necessarily contained a romantic or sexual dimension.[50] Other forms of physical intimacy include affectionate hugs, kisses, and even struggles. Companions who have endured physical challenges together—in athletics or emergencies, for example—form a bond that can last a lifetime.

In other cases, intimacy comes from *intellectual* sharing. Not every exchange of ideas counts as intimacy, of course. Talking about next week's midterm with your professor or classmates isn't likely to forge strong relational bonds. But when you engage another person in an exchange of important ideas, a kind of closeness develops that can be powerful and exciting.

A third quality of intimacy is *emotion:* exchanging important feelings. This chapter will offer several guidelines for disclosing your thoughts and feelings to others. If you follow those guidelines, you will probably recognize a qualitative change in your relationships.

If we define *intimacy* as being close to another person, then *shared activities* can provide another way to achieve this state. Shared activities can include everything from working side by side at a job to meeting regularly for exercise workouts. Although shared activities are no guarantee of intimacy, people who spend time together can develop unique ways of relating that transform the relationship from an impersonal

one that could be done with anybody to one with interpersonal qualities. For example, both friendships and romantic relationships are often characterized by several forms of play. Partners invent private codes, fool around by acting like other people, tease one another, and play games—everything from having punning contests to arm wrestling.[51]

CULTURAL IDIOM
fool around:
spend time joking

Some intimate relationships exhibit all four qualities: physical intimacy, intellectual exchanges, emotional disclosure, and shared activities. Other intimate relationships exhibit only one or two. Some relationships, of course, aren't intimate in any way. Acquaintances, roommates, and coworkers may never become intimate. In some cases even family members develop smooth but relatively impersonal relationships.

Not even the closest relationships always operate at the highest level of intimacy. At some times you might share all of your thoughts or feelings with a friend, family member, or lover, and at other times you might withdraw. You might freely share your feelings about one topic and stay more aloof in another one. The same principle holds for physical intimacy, which waxes and wanes in most relationships. The dialectical view of relational maintenance described later in this chapter explains how intimacy can wax and wane, even in the closest relationships.

Male and Female Intimacy Styles

Until recently most social scientists believed that women are better at developing and maintaining intimate relationships than men.[52] This belief grew from the assumption that the disclosure of personal information is the most important ingredient of intimacy. Most research *does* show that women (taken as a group, of course) are more willing than men to share their thoughts and feelings.[53] In terms of the amount and depth of information exchanged, female-female relationships are at the top of the disclosure list. Male-female relationships come in second, whereas relationships between men have less disclosure than any other type. At every age, women disclose more than men, and the information they disclose is more personal and more likely to involve feelings. Although both sexes are equally likely to reveal negative information, men are less likely to share positive feelings.[54]

Through the mid-1980s many social scientists interpreted the relative lack of male self-disclosure as a sign that men are unwilling or even unable to develop close relationships. Some argued that the female trait of disclosing personal information and feelings makes them more "emotionally mature" and "interpersonally competent" than men. Personal growth programs and self-help books urge men to achieve closeness by learning to open up and share their feelings.

Scholarship conducted in roughly the last two decades has begun to show that male-female differences aren't as great as they seem,[55] and emotional expression isn't the

CULTURAL IDIOM
to open up:
talk about subjects that otherwise might be withheld

Sally Forth

Source: Reprinted by special permission of King Features Syndicate.

only way to develop close relationships. Unlike women, who value personal talk, men grow close to one another by doing things together. In one study more than 75 percent of the men surveyed said that their most meaningful experiences with friends came from activities other than talking.[56] They reported that through shared activities they "grew on one another," developed feelings of interdependence, showed appreciation for one another, and demonstrated mutual liking. Likewise, men regarded practical help from other men as a measure of caring. Research like this shows that, for many men, closeness grows from activities that don't depend heavily on disclosure: A friend is a person who does things *for* you and *with* you.

The difference between male and female measures of intimacy helps explain some of the stresses and misunderstandings that can arise between the sexes. For example, a woman who looks for emotional disclosure as a measure of affection may overlook an "inexpressive" man's efforts to show he cares by doing favors or spending time together. Fixing a leaky faucet or taking a hike may look like ways to avoid getting close, but to the man who proposes them they may be measures of affection and bids for intimacy. Likewise, differing ideas about the timing and meaning of sex can lead to misunderstandings. Whereas many women think of sex as a way to express intimacy that has already developed, men are more likely to see it as a way to *create* that intimacy.[57] In this sense, the man who encourages sex early in a relationship or after a fight may not just be a testosterone-crazed lecher: He may view the shared activity as a way to build closeness. By contrast, the woman who views personal talk as the pathway to intimacy may resist the idea of physical closeness before the emotional side of the relationship has been discussed.

Cultural Influences on Intimacy

The notion of how much intimacy is desirable and how to express it varies from one culture to another.[58] In one study, researchers asked residents of Great Britain, Japan, Hong Kong, and Italy to describe their use of 33 rules that governed interaction in a wide range of communication behaviors: everything from the use of humor to hand shaking to the management of money.[59] The results showed that the greatest differences between Asian and European cultures focused on the rules for dealing with intimacy: showing emotions, expressing affection in public, engaging in sexual activity, respecting privacy, and so on. Culture also plays a role in shaping how much intimacy we seek in different types of relationships. For instance, the Japanese seem to expect more intimacy in friendships, whereas Americans look for more intimacy in romantic relationships with a boy- or girlfriend, fiancée, or spouse.[60]

In some collectivist cultures such as Taiwan and Japan there is an especially great difference in the way members communicate with members of their "in-groups" (such as family and close friends) and with those they view as outsiders.[61] They generally do not reach out to strangers, often waiting until they are properly introduced before entering into a conversation. Once introduced, they address outsiders with a degree of formality. They go to extremes to hide unfavorable information about in-group members from outsiders, on the principle that one doesn't wash dirty laundry in public. By contrast, members of more individualistic cultures like the United States and Australia make less of a distinction between personal relationships and casual ones. They act more familiar with strangers and disclose more personal information, making them excellent "cocktail party conversationalists."

Within American culture, intimacy varies from one group to another. For example, working-class black men are much more disclosing than their white counterparts.[62] By contrast, upwardly mobile black men communicate more like white men with the same social agenda, disclosing less with their male friends.

CULTURAL IDIOM

wash dirty laundry in public: disclose personal and private problems and concerns beyond one's family or group

Self-Disclosure in Interpersonal Relationships

"We don't have any secrets," some people proudly claim. Opening up certainly is important. Earlier in this chapter you learned that one ingredient in qualitatively interpersonal relationships is disclosure. You've also read that we find others more attractive when they share certain private information with us. Given the obvious importance of self-disclosure, we need to take a closer look at the subject. Just what is it? When is it desirable? How can it best be done?

The best place to begin is with a definition. **Self-disclosure** is the process of deliberately revealing information about oneself that is significant and that would not normally be known by others. Let's take a closer look at some parts of this definition. Self-disclosure must be *deliberate*. If you accidentally mentioned to a friend that you were thinking about quitting a job or proposing marriage, that information would not fit into the category we are examining here. Self-disclosure must also be *significant*. Revealing relatively trivial information—the fact that you like fudge, for example—does not qualify as self-disclosure. The third requirement is that the information being revealed would *not be known by others*. There's nothing noteworthy about telling others that you are depressed or elated if they already know how you're feeling.

As Table 6-1 shows, people self-disclose for a variety of reasons. Some involve developing and maintaining relationships, but other reasons often drive revealing personal information. The reasons for disclosing vary from one situation to another, depending on several factors. The first important factor in whether we disclose

"There's something you need to know about me, Donna. I don't like people knowing things about me."

CULTURAL IDIOM

opening up:
talking about subjects that might otherwise be kept private

TABLE 6-1   Reasons for Self-Disclosure

Self-disclosure has the potential to improve and expand interpersonal relationships, but it serves other functions as well. As you read each of the following reasons why people reveal themselves, see which apply to you.

Reason	Example/Explanation
Catharsis	"I need to get this off my chest . . ."
Self-clarification	"I'm really confused about something I did last night. If I tell you, maybe I can figure out why I did it . . ."
Self-validation	"I think I did the right thing. Let me tell you why I did it . . ."
Reciprocity	"I really like you . . ." (Hoping for a similar disclosure by other person.)
Impression management	Salesperson to customer: "My boss would kill me for giving you this discount . . ." (Hoping disclosure will build trust.)
Relationship maintenance and enhancement	"I'm worried about the way things are going between us. Let's talk." *or* "I sure am glad we're together!"
Control	(Employee to boss, hoping to get raise) "I got a job offer yesterday from our biggest competitor."

Adapted from V. J. Derlega and J. Grezlak, "Appropriateness of Self-Disclosure," in G. J. Chelune, ed., *Self-Disclosure* (San Francisco, CA: Jossey-Bass, 1979).

MEDIA ROOM
Self-Disclosure in Personal Relationships

With its potential for dramatic moments, self-disclosure is a frequent theme in films and television shows. The examples here illustrate both the value and pitfalls of revealing personal information.

Little Miss Sunshine chronicles the adventures of seven-year old Olive (Abigail Breslin) and her dysfunctional family as they drive her cross-country to compete in a beauty contest. Olive's father, mother, brother, uncle, and grandfather are so burdened with quirks and neuroses that making it to California sane, alive, and on time is always in doubt. In the face of many challenges, the family members begin to share closely held personal secrets—and in so doing grow closer.

On the eve of transgender surgery, Bree (Felicity Huffman) discovers that she/he is the parent of a fifteen-year old delinquent who was conceived in a long-ago one-night stand. The film *Transamerica* centers on Bree's evolving relationship with the son she never knew she had. It's an understatement to say that increasingly personal and important self-disclosures change the nature of their relationship.

In *Meet the Fockers*, Greg Focker (Ben Stiller) and fiancée Pam Byrnes (Teri Polo) arrange a weekend getaway to introduce their very different parents to each other. Unlike the reserved Jack and Dina Byrnes (Robert De Niro and Blythe Danner), Greg's zany mother and father (Barbra Streisand and Dustin Hoffman) revel in sharing anything and everything about their personal lives—with predictably disastrous results. While this film is a lighthearted comedy, it does show the importance of reciprocity in self-disclosure.

Nine years earlier, American Jesse (Ethan Hawke) and Parisian Celine (Julie Delpy) spent an intensely romantic twelve hours in Vienna (depicted in the film *Before Sunrise*). In the film *Before Sunset*, they meet again in a Paris bookstore and use the few available hours to reconnect. At first, Jesse and Celine banter superficially, then they slowly and cautiously begin to open up. Over and over they touch on a risky topic, then back off with a joke. This film captures the nervous hesitations, false starts, confessions, and retreats that occur when revealing important information to people who matter.

Almost every episode of the popular television series *Desperate Housewives* involves an abundance of self-disclosure between the fictional residents of Wisteria Lane. The neighbors disclose—to a fault—their romantic interests, dreams, flaws, and indiscretions to one another. Many of these revelations show that self-disclosure has the potential to damage relationships.

Little Miss Sunshine (2006, Rated R)

Transamerica (2006, Rated R)

Meet the Fockers (2004, Rated PG-13)

Before Sunset (2004, Rated R)

Desperate Housewives (2004– , Rated TV-PG)

For more film and television suggestions, see *Now Playing* at the *Understanding Human Communication* website at www.oup.com/us/uhc10.

seems to be how well we know the other person.[63] When the target of disclosure is a friend, the most frequent reason people give for volunteering personal information is relationship maintenance and enhancement. The second important reason is self-clarification—to sort out confusion, to understand ourselves better.

With strangers, reciprocity becomes the most common reason for disclosing. We offer information about ourselves to strangers to learn more about them, so we can decide whether and how to continue the relationship. The second most common reason is impression formation. We often reveal information about ourselves to strangers to make ourselves look good. This information, of course, is usually positive—at least in the early stages of a friendship.

Models of Self-Disclosure

Over several decades, social scientists have created various models to represent and understand how self-disclosure operates in relationships. In the next few pages we will look at two of the best-known models.

Breadth and Depth: Social Penetration   Social psychologists Irwin Altman and Dalmas Taylor describe two ways in which communication can be more or less disclosing.[64] Their **social penetration model** is pictured in Figure 6-3. The first dimension of self-disclosure in this model involves the **breadth** of information volunteered—the range of subjects being discussed. For example, the breadth of disclosure in your relationship with a fellow worker will expand as you begin revealing information about your life away from the job, as well as on-the-job details. The second dimension of disclosure is the **depth** of the information being volunteered, the shift from relatively nonrevealing messages to more personal ones.

Depending on the breadth and depth of information shared, a relationship can be defined as casual or intimate. In a casual relationship, the breadth may be great, but not the depth. A more intimate relationship is likely to have high depth in at least one area. The most intimate relationships are those in which disclosure is great in both breadth and depth. Altman and Taylor see the development of a relationship as a progression from the periphery of their model to its center, a process that typically occurs over time. Each of your personal relationships probably has a different combination of breadth of subjects and depth of disclosure. Figure 6-4 pictures a student's self-disclosure in one relationship.

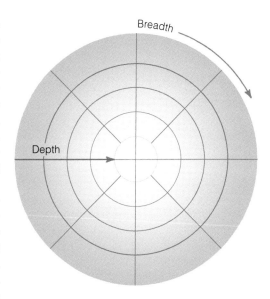

FIGURE 6-3   Social Penetration Model

What makes the disclosure in some messages deeper than others? One way to measure depth is by how far it goes on two of the dimensions that define self-disclosure. Some revelations are certainly more *significant* than others. Consider the difference between saying "I love my family" and "I love you." Other statements qualify as deep disclosure because they are *private*. Sharing a secret you've told to only a few close friends is certainly an act of self-disclosure, but it's even more revealing to divulge information that you've never told anyone.

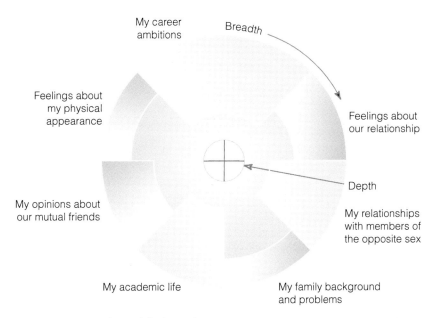

FIGURE 6-4   Sample Model of Social Penetration

Self-Disclosure, Self-Awareness, and Relational Quality   Another model that helps represent how self-disclosure operates is the **Johari Window**.[65] (The window takes its name from the first names of its creators, Joseph Luft and Harry Ingham.) Imagine a frame inside which is everything there is to know about you: your likes and dislikes, your goals, your secrets, your needs—everything. (See Figure 6-5.)

Of course, you aren't aware of everything about yourself. Like most people, you're probably discovering new things about yourself all the time. To represent this, we can divide the frame containing everything about you into two parts: the part you know about and the part you don't know about, as in Figure 6-6.

We can also divide this frame containing everything about you in another way. In this division the first part contains the things about you that others know, and the second part contains the things about you that you keep to yourself. Figure 6-7 represents this view.

When we impose these two divided frames one atop the other, we have a Johari Window. By looking at Figure 6-8 you can see the *everything about you* window divided into four parts.

Part 1 represents the information of which both you and the other person are aware. This part is your *open area*. Part 2 represents the *blind area:* information of which you are unaware but the other person knows. You learn about information in the blind area primarily through feedback. Part 3 represents your *hidden area:* information that you know but aren't willing to reveal to others. Items in this hidden area become public primarily through self-disclosure, which is the focus of this chapter. Part 4 represents information that is *unknown* to both you and others. At first, the unknown area seems impossible to verify. After all, if neither you nor others know what it contains, how can you be sure it exists? We can deduce its existence because we are constantly discovering new things about ourselves. It is not unusual to discover, for example, that you have an unrecognized talent, strength, or weakness. Items move from the unknown area into the open area either directly when you disclose your insight or through one of the other areas first.

Interpersonal relationships of any depth are virtually impossible if the individuals involved have little open area. Going a step further, you can see that a relationship is limited by the individual who is less open, that is, who possesses the smaller open area. Figure 6-9 illustrates this situation with Johari Windows. A's window is set up in reverse so that A's and B's open areas are adjacent. Notice that the amount of communication (represented by the arrows connecting the two open areas) is dictated by the

FIGURE 6-5   The Johari Window: Everything about You

FIGURE 6-6   The Johari Window: Known to Self; Not Known to Self

FIGURE 6-7   The Johari Window: Known to Others; Not Known to Others

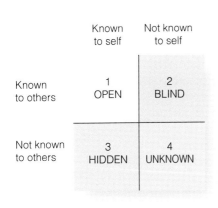

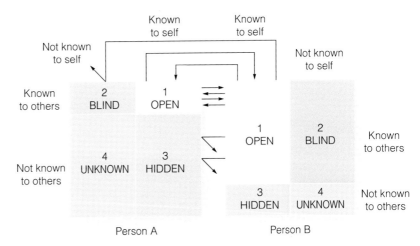

FIGURE 6-8   The Johari Window: Open; Blind; Hidden; Unknown

FIGURE 6-9   The Johari Window: Self-Disclosure Levels in Two-Way Communication

size of the smaller open area of A. The arrows originating from B's open area and being turned aside by A's hidden and blind areas represent unsuccessful attempts to communicate.

You have probably found yourself in situations that resemble Figure 6-9. Perhaps you have felt the frustration of not being able to get to know someone who was too reserved. Perhaps you have blocked another person's attempts to build a relationship with you in the same way. Whether you picture yourself more like Person A or Person B, the fact is that self-disclosure on both sides is necessary for the development of any interpersonal relationship. This chapter will describe just how much self-disclosure is optimal and of what type.

Characteristics of Effective Self-Disclosure

Self-disclosure can certainly be valuable, but using it effectively requires an understanding of how it operates. Here are some findings from researchers that will help you decide when and how disclosure works best.

Self-Disclosure Is Influenced by Culture   The level of self-disclosure that is appropriate in one culture may seem completely inappropriate in another one. Disclosure is especially high in mainstream North American society. In fact, natives of the United States are more disclosing than members of any other culture studied.[66] They are likely to disclose more about themselves to acquaintances and even strangers. By contrast, Germans tend to disclose little about themselves except in intimate relationships with a select few, and Japanese reveal very little about themselves in even their closest relationships.

Cultural differences like this mean that what counts as disclosing communication varies from one culture to another. If you were raised in the United States, you might view people from certain other cultures as undisclosing or even standoffish. But the amount of personal information that the nonnatives reveal might actually be quite personal and revealing according to the standards of their culture. The converse is also true: To members of some other cultures, North Americans probably appear like exhibitionists who spew personal information to anyone within earshot.

CULTURAL IDIOM

standoffish:
unfriendly

earshot:
the distance at which one can hear something or someone

When communicating with people from different cultures it's important to consider their standards for appropriate disclosure. Don't mistakenly judge them according to your own standards. Likewise, be sensitive about honoring their standards when talking about yourself. In this sense, choosing the proper level of self-disclosure isn't too different from choosing the appropriate way of dressing or eating when encountering members of a different culture: What seems familiar and correct at home may not be suitable with strangers. As you read on, realize that the characteristics and guidelines that suit mainstream North American culture may not apply in other contexts.

Self-Disclosure Usually Occurs in Dyads   Although it is possible for people to disclose a great deal about themselves in groups, such communication usually occurs in one-to-one settings. Because revealing significant information about yourself involves a certain amount of risk, limiting the disclosure to one person at a time minimizes the chance that your disclosure will lead to unhappy consequences.

Effective Self-Disclosure Is Usually Symmetrical   Note in Figure 6-9 that the amount of successful, two-way communication (represented by the arrows connecting the two open areas) is dictated by the size of the smaller open area of A. The arrows that are originating from B's open area and being turned aside by A's hidden and blind areas represent unsuccessful attempts to communicate. In situations such as this, it's easy to imagine how B would soon limit the amount of disclosure to match that of A. On the other hand, if A were willing to match the degree of disclosure given by B, the relationship would move to a new level of intimacy. In either case, we can expect that most often the degree of disclosure between partners will soon stabilize at a symmetrical level.

Effective Self-Disclosure Occurs Incrementally   Although instances occur in which partners start their relationship by telling everything about themselves to each other, such cases are rare. In most cases, the amount of disclosure increases over time. We begin relationships by revealing relatively little about ourselves; then if our first bits of self-disclosure are well received and bring on similar responses from the other person, we're willing to reveal more. This principle is important to remember. It would usually be a mistake to assume that the way to build a strong relationship would be to reveal the most private details about yourself when first making contact with another person. Unless the circumstances are unique, such baring of your soul would be likely to scare potential partners away rather than bring them closer.

Self-Disclosure Is Relatively Scarce   Most conversations—even among friends—focus on everyday mundane topics and disclose little or no personal information.[67] Even partners in intimate relationships rarely talk about personal information.[68] Whether or not we open up to others is based on several criteria, some of which are listed in Table 6-2.

What is the optimal amount of self-disclosure? You might suspect that the correct answer is "the more, the better," at least in personal relationships. Research has showed that the matter isn't this simple, however.[69] For example, there seems to be a curvilinear relationship between openness and satisfaction in marriage, so that a moderate amount of openness produces better results than either extreme disclosure or withholding. One good measure of happiness is how well the level of disclosure matches the expectations of communicators: If we get what we believe is a reasonable amount of candor from others, we are happy. If they tell us too little—or even too much—we become less satisfied.

TABLE 6-2   Some Criteria Used to Reveal Family Secrets

Intimate Exchange
Does the other person have a similar problem?
Would knowing the secret help the other person feel better?
Would knowing the secret help the other person manage his or her problem?

Exposure
Will the other person find out this information, even if I don't tell him or her?
Is the other person asking me directly to reveal this information?

Urgency
Is it very important that the other person know this information?
Will revealing this information make matters better?

Acceptance
Will the other person still accept me if I reveal this information?

Conversational Appropriateness
Will my disclosure fit into the conversation?
Has the topic of my disclosure come up in this conversation?

Relational Security
Do I trust the other person with this information?
Do I feel close enough to this person to reveal the secret?

Important Reason
Is there a pressing reason to reveal this information?

Permission
Have other people involved in the secret given their permission for me to reveal it?
Would I feel okay telling the people involved that I have revealed the secret?

Membership
Is the person to whom I'm revealing the secret going to join this group (i.e., family)?

Adapted from A. L. Vangelisti, J. P. Caughlin, and L. Timmerman, "Criteria for Revealing Family Secrets," *Communication Monographs* 68 (2001): 1–27.

Guidelines for Appropriate Self-Disclosure

One fear we've had while writing this chapter is that a few overenthusiastic readers may throw down their books and begin to share every personal detail of their lives with whomever they can find. As you can imagine, this kind of behavior isn't an example of effective interpersonal communication.

No single style of self-disclosure is appropriate for every situation. Let's take a look at some guidelines that can help you recognize how to express yourself in a way that's rewarding for you and the others involved.[70]

Is the Other Person Important to You?   There are several ways in which someone might be important. Perhaps you have an ongoing relationship deep enough so that sharing significant parts of yourself justifies keeping your present level of togetherness intact. Or perhaps the person to whom you're considering disclosing is someone with whom you've previously related on a less personal level. But now you see a chance to grow closer, and disclosure may be the path toward developing that personal relationship.

CULTURAL IDIOM

opening yourself up:
letting yourself become vulnerable

to bite your tongue:
to remain silent

in the same vein:
related to this idea

Is the Risk of Disclosing Reasonable? Take a realistic look at the potential risks of self-disclosure. Even if the probable benefits are great, opening yourself up to almost certain rejection may be asking for trouble. For instance, it might be foolhardy to share your important feelings with someone you know is likely to betray your confidences or ridicule them. On the other hand, knowing that your partner is trustworthy and supportive makes the prospect of speaking out more reasonable.

Revealing personal thoughts and feelings can be especially risky on the job.[71] The politics of the workplace sometimes requires communicators to keep feelings to themselves in order to accomplish both personal and organizational goals. You might, for example, find the opinions of a boss or customer personally offensive but decide to bite your tongue rather than risk your job or lose goodwill for the company.

Are the Amount and Type of Disclosure Appropriate? A third point to realize is that there are degrees of self-disclosure. Telling others about yourself isn't an all-or-nothing decision you must make. It's possible to share some facts, opinions, or feelings with one person while reserving riskier ones for others. In the same vein, before sharing very important information with someone who does matter to you, you might consider testing reactions by disclosing less personal data.

Is the Disclosure Relevant to the Situation at Hand? The kind of disclosure that is often a characteristic of highly personal relationships usually isn't appropriate in less personal settings. For instance, a study of classroom communication revealed that sharing all feelings—both positive and negative—and being completely honest resulted in less cohesiveness than having a "relatively" honest climate in which pleasant but superficial relationships were the norm.[72]

Even in personal relationships—with close friends, family members, and so on—constant disclosure isn't a useful goal. The level of sharing in successful relationships rises and falls in cycles. You may go through a period of great disclosure and then spend another period of relative nondisclosure. Even during a phase of high disclosure, sharing *everything* about yourself isn't necessarily constructive. Usually the subject of appropriate self-disclosure involves the relationship rather than personal information.

Is the Disclosure Reciprocated? There's nothing quite as disconcerting as talking your heart out to someone only to discover that the other person has yet to say anything to you that is half as revealing as what you've been saying. Unequal self-disclosure creates an unbalanced relationship, one doomed to fall apart.

There are few times when one-way disclosure is acceptable. Most of them involve formal, therapeutic relationships in which a client approaches a trained professional with the goal of resolving a problem. For instance, you wouldn't necessarily expect to hear about a physician's personal ailments during a visit to a medical office. Nonetheless, it's interesting to note that one frequently noted characteristic of effective psychotherapists, counselors, and teachers is a willingness to share their feelings about a relationship with their clients.

Will the Effect Be Constructive? Self-disclosure can be a vicious tool if it's not used carefully. Psychologist George Bach suggests that every person has a psychological "belt line." Below that belt line are areas about which the person is extremely sensitive. Bach says that jabbing at a "below-the-belt" area is a surefire way to disable another person, although usually at great cost to the relationship. It's important to consider the effects of your candor before opening up to others. Comments such as "I've always thought you were pretty unintelligent" or "Last year I made love to your best friend" *may* sometimes resolve old business and thus be constructive, but they also can be devastating—to the listener, to the relationship, and to your self-esteem.

CULTURAL IDIOM

talking your heart out:
revealing your innermost thoughts
and feelings

Is the Self-Disclosure Clear and Understandable?   When you express yourself to others, it's important that you share yourself in a way that's intelligible. This means describing the *sources* of your message clearly. For instance, it's far better to describe another's behavior by saying "When you don't answer my phone calls or drop by to visit anymore . . ." than to complain vaguely, "When you avoid me. . . ."

It's also vital to express your *thoughts* and *feelings* explicitly. "I feel worried because I'm afraid you don't care about me" is more understandable than "I don't like the way things have been going."

Alternatives to Self-Disclosure

At first glance, our moral heritage leads us to abhor anything less than the truth. Ethicists point out that the very existence of a society seems based on a foundation of truthfulness.[73] Although isolated cultures do exist where deceit is a norm, they are dysfunctional and on the verge of breakdown.

Although honesty is desirable in principle, it often has risky, potentially unpleasant consequences. This explains why communicators—even those with the best intentions—aren't always completely honest when they find themselves in situations when honesty would be uncomfortable.[74] Three common alternatives to self-disclosure are lies, equivocation, and hinting. We will take a closer look at each one.

Lies   To most people, lying appears to be a breach of ethics. Although lying to gain unfair advantage over an unknowing victim seems clearly wrong, another kind of untruth isn't so easy to dismiss as completely unethical. White lies, more appropriately called **altruistic lies,** are defined (at least by the people who tell them) as being harmless, or even helpful, to the person to whom they are told.[75] As Table 6-3 shows, at least some of the lies we tell are indeed intended to be helpful, or at least relatively benign.

Whether or not they are innocent, altruistic lies are certainly common. In one study, 130 subjects were asked to keep track of the truthfulness of their everyday conversational statements.[76] Only 38.5 percent of these statements—slightly more than a third—proved to be totally honest. In another experiment, 147 people between the ages of 18 and 71 kept a log of all the lies they told over a one-week period. Both

TABLE 6-3 Some Reasons for Lying

Reason	Example
Acquire resources	"Oh, please let me add this class. If I don't get in, I'll never graduate on time!"
Protect resources	"I'd like to lend you the money, but I'm short myself."
Initiate and continue interaction	"Excuse me, I'm lost. Do you live around here?"
Avoid conflict	"It's not a big deal. We can do it your way. Really."
Avoid interaction or take leave	"That sounds like fun, but I'm busy Saturday night." "Oh, look what time it is! I've got to run!"
Present a competent image	"Sure, I understand. No problem."
Increase social desirability	"Yeah, I've done a fair amount of skiing."

Adapted from categories originally presented in C. Camden, M. T. Motley, and A. Wilson, "White Lies in Interpersonal Communication: A Taxonomy and Preliminary Investigation of Social Motivations," *Western Journal of Speech Communication* 48 (1984): 315.

CULTURAL IDIOM

a put-on:
a false show of emotion

men and women reported being untruthful in approximately a fifth of their conversations that lasted over ten minutes.[77] Over the course of the week, the subjects reported lying to about 30 percent of the people with whom they had one-on-one conversations. The rate was much higher in some relationships. For example, dating couples lie to each other in about a third of their interactions, and college students told at least one lie to their mothers in fully 50 percent of their conversations. In yet another study, subjects recorded their conversations over a two-day period and later counted their own deceptions. The average lie rate: three fibs for every ten minutes of conversation.[78]

What are the consequences of discovering that you've been lied to? In an interpersonal relationship, the discovery can be traumatic. As we grow closer to others, our expectations about their honesty grow stronger. After all, discovering that you've been deceived requires you to redefine not only the lie you just uncovered, but also many of the messages you previously took for granted. Was last week's compliment really sincere? Was your joke really funny, or was the other person's laughter a put-on? Does the other person care about you as much as he or she claimed?

Research has shown that deception does, in fact, threaten relationships.[79] Not all lies are equally devastating, however. Feelings like dismay and betrayal are greatest when the relationship is most intense, when the importance of the subject is high, and when there was previous suspicion that the other person wasn't being completely honest. Of these three factors, the importance of the information lied about proved to be the key factor in provoking a relational crisis. We may be able to cope with "misdemeanor" lying, but "felonies" are a grave threat. In fact, the discovery of major deception can lead to the end of the relationship. More than two-thirds of the subjects in one study reported that their relationship had ended since they discovered a lie. Furthermore, they attributed the breakup directly to the lie. If preserving a relationship is important, honesty—at least about important matters—really does appear to be the best policy.

Equivocation   Lying isn't the only alternative to self-disclosure. When faced with the choice between lying and telling an unpleasant truth, communicators can—and often do—equivocate. As Chapter 3 explained, **equivocal language** has two or more equally plausible meanings. Sometimes people send equivocal messages without meaning to, resulting in confusion. "I'll meet you at the apartment," could refer to more than one place. But other times we are deliberately vague. For instance, when a friend

Source: © Zits Partnership. Reprinted with special permission of King Features Syndicate.

INVITATION TO INSIGHT
Is It Ever Right to Lie?

Is it ever right to lie? What about the example from freshman philosophy: The Nazis come to your door asking if you are hiding a Jewish family. You are. Should you say "No"? Or, on a mundane level, your spouse or lover walks in with an utterly silly new hairdo and asks, "Do you like it?" Does morality dictate that you ruin the evening? Or can you, in both cases, finesse the answer, not lying but not telling the truth, either, perhaps by avoiding an answer to the question?

The demand for honesty is contextual. It depends on what the truth concerns. The Bible tells us not to bear false witness against our neighbor. Perjury, we can agree, is wrong: The consequences can be awful. But it seems to me absolutely crucial to distinguish here between public and private life. Perjury, by its very nature, is public, as is politics. Sex, with a few obvious exceptions, is part of our private life. And just about everyone is less than forthright about sex.

Not all untruths are malicious. Telling the truth can complicate or destroy social relationships. It can undermine precious collective myths. Honesty can be cruel. Sometimes, deception is not a vice but a social virtue, and systematic deception is an essential part of the order of the (social) world.

In many countries—Japan and Western Samoa, for example—social harmony is valued far more than truthfulness as such. To tell another person what he or she wants to hear, rather than what one might actually feel or believe, is not only permitted but expected. Could we not begin to see our own enlightened emphasis on "seeking the truth at all costs" as one more ethnocentric peculiarity, another curious product of our strong sense of individualism, and a dangerously unsociable conception?

The obvious truth is that our simplest social relationships could not exist without the opaque medium of the lie. The best answer to the question "What are you thinking?" is often "Oh,

nothing." Perhaps deception, not truth, is the cement of civilization—cement that does not so much hold us together as safely separate us and our thoughts. Some things are better left in the dark.

In contrast to Kant, for whom the rule against lying was a moral law, a "categorical imperative" never to be overridden, utilitarian philosophers insist that lying is wrong only because a lie does, in fact, cause more harm than good. There is no absolute prohibition here, rather perhaps a "rule of thumb," and there may well be many cases, such as the "white lies" described above, in which lying causes no harm and may even be commendable. The problem, as Nietzsche so wisely complains, is "not that you lied to me, but that I no longer believe you." It is not the breach of the principle against lying that is so troublesome, nor is it the consequences of the lie or the character of the liar. It is that lying compromises and corrupts our relationships.

In other words, the wrongness of lying does not have to do primarily with breaches of principle or miscalculations of harm and good. Lying is wrong because it constitutes a breach of trust, which is not a principle but a very particular and personal relationship between people.

What is wrong with lying, in other words, is not exactly what philosophers have often supposed. Lying undermines relationships by undermining trust. But trust may just as often be supported by mutual myths, by religious faith, by a clear understanding of what is private and personal and what is "the public's right to know." Trust is usually violated by lies, but trust can be more deeply damaged by a violation of personal boundaries, which in turn may invite lies and deception to protect what has been violated.

Robert C. Solomon

asks what you think of an awful outfit, you could say, "It's really unusual—one of a kind!" Likewise, if you are too angry to accept a friend's apology but don't want to appear petty, you might say, "Don't mention it."

The value of equivocation becomes clear when you consider the alternatives. Consider the dilemma of what to say when you've been given an unwanted present—an ugly painting, for example—and the giver asks what you think of it. How can you respond? On the one hand, you need to choose between telling the truth and lying. On the other hand, you have a choice of whether to make your response clear or vague. Figure 6-10 displays these choices. After considering the alternatives, it's clear that the first choice—an equivocal, true response—is far preferable to the other choices in several respects. First, it spares the receiver from embarrassment. For example, rather than flatly saying "no" to an unappealing invitation, it may be kinder to say "I have other plans"—even if those plans are to stay home and watch television.

Besides saving face for the recipient, honest equivocation can be less stressful for the sender than either telling the truth bluntly or lying. Because equivocation is often easier to take than the cold, hard truth, it spares the teller from feeling guilty. It's less taxing on the conscience to say "I've never tasted anything like this" than to say "this meal tastes terrible," even though the latter comment is more precise. Few people *want* to lie, and equivocation provides an alternative to deceit.[80]

A study by communication researcher Sandra Metts and her colleagues shows how equivocation can save face in difficult situations.[81] Several hundred college students were asked how they would turn down the unwanted sexual overtures from a person whose feelings were important to them: either a close friend, a prospective date, or a dating partner. The majority of students chose a diplomatic reaction ("I just don't think I'm ready for this right now") as being more face saving and comfortable than a direct statement like "I just don't feel sexually attracted to you." The diplomatic reaction seemed sufficiently clear to get the message across but not so blunt as to embarrass or even humiliate the other person. (Interestingly, men said they would be able to handle a direct rejection more comfortably than women. The researchers suggest that one reason for the difference is that men stereotypically initiate sexual offers and thus are more likely to expect rejection.)

Besides preventing embarrassment, equivocal language can also save the speaker from being caught lying. If a potential employer asks about your grades during a job interview, you would be safe saying, "I had a B average last semester," even though your overall grade average is closer to C. The statement isn't a complete answer, but it is honest as far as it goes. As one team of researchers put it, "Equivocation is neither a false message nor a clear truth, but rather an alternative used precisely when both of these are to be avoided."[82]

Given these advantages, it's not surprising that most people will usually choose to equivocate rather than tell a lie. In a series of experiments, subjects chose between telling a face-saving lie, telling the truth, and equivocating. Only 6 percent chose the lie, and between 3 and 4 percent chose the hurtful truth. By contrast, over 90 percent chose the equivocal response.[83] People *say* they prefer truth-telling to equivocating,[84] but given the choice, they prefer to finesse the truth.

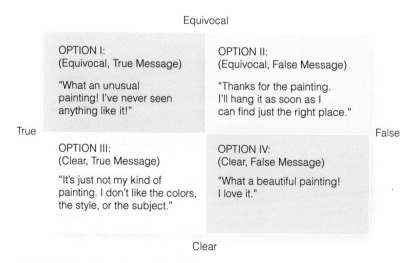

FIGURE 6-10   Dimensions of Truthfulness and Equivocation

Hinting   Hints are more direct than equivocal statements. Whereas an equivocal message isn't necessarily aimed at changing others' behavior, a hint seeks to get the desired response from others. Some hints are designed to save the receiver from embarrassment:[85]

FACE-SAVING HINT	DIRECT STATEMENT
These desserts are terribly overpriced.	You're too overweight to be ordering dessert.
I know you're busy; I'd better let you go.	I'm bored. I want to get out of this conversation.

Other hints are strategies for saving the sender from embarrassment:

FACE-SAVING HINT	DIRECT STATEMENT
I'm pretty sure that smoking isn't permitted here.	Your smoking bothers me.
Gee, it's almost lunchtime. Have you ever eaten at that new Italian restaurant around the corner?	I'd like to invite you out for lunch, but I don't want to risk a "no" answer to my invitation.

The success of a hint depends on the other person's ability to pick up the unexpressed message. Your subtle remarks might go right over the head of an insensitive receiver—or one who chooses not to respond to them. If this does happen, you still have the choice to be more direct. If the costs of a straightforward message seem too high, you can withdraw without risk.

It's easy to see why people choose hints, equivocations, and white lies instead of complete self-disclosure. These strategies provide a way to manage difficult situations that is easier than the alternatives for both the speaker and the receiver of the message. In this sense, successful liars, equivocators, and hinters can be said to possess a certain kind of communicative competence. On the other hand, there are certainly times when honesty is the right approach, even if it's painful. At times like these, evaders could be viewed as lacking the competence or the integrity to handle a situation most effectively.

Are hints, benign lies, and equivocations an ethical alternative to self-disclosure? Some of the examples in these pages suggest the answer is a qualified "yes." Many social scientists and philosophers agree. Some argue that the morality of a speaker's *motives* for lying ought to be judged, not the deceptive act itself.[86] Others ask whether the *effects* of a lie will be worth the deception. Ethicist Sissela Bok offers some circumstances where deception may be justified: doing good, avoiding harm, and protecting a larger truth.[87] Perhaps the right questions to ask, then, are whether an indirect message is truly in the interests of the receiver, and whether this sort of evasion is the only effective way to behave. Bok suggests another way to check the justifiability of a lie: Imagine how others would respond if they knew what you were really thinking or feeling. Would they accept your reasons for not disclosing?

CULTURAL IDIOM

to pick up:
to understand

go right over the head of:
fail to be understood by

ETHICAL CHALLENGE

● **The Ethics of Lying and Equivocating**

Research shows that virtually everyone hints, lies, and equivocates for a variety of reasons. Explore the ethical legitimacy of your lies and equivocations by following these directions:

1. For a two-day period, keep track of:

   a. Your hints, lies, and equivocations.

   b. Your reason for taking one of these approaches in each situation.

   c. The positive and negative consequences (for you and the other person) of avoiding self-disclosure.

2. Based on your analysis of the information collected in Step 1, identify the ethical legitimacy of each type of nondisclosing communication. Are any sorts of deception justifiable? Which sorts are not? How would you feel if you discovered the other person had not been straightforward with you under similar circumstances?

Summary

An interpersonal relationship is one in which two or more people meet one another's social needs to a greater or lesser degree. We form these relationships for a variety of reasons. Some of these reasons are rather straightforward (e.g., proximity, appearance, rewards) while others involve what can informally be called "chemistry" (e.g., similarity, mutual self-disclosure, reciprocal attraction).

Communication can be considered interpersonal according to either the context or the quality of interaction. Qualitatively interpersonal communication can occur both face to face and in mediated relationships. Communication in relationships consists of both content and relational messages. Explicit relational messages are termed *metacommunication*.

Some communication theorists suggest that intimate relationships pass through a series of stages, each of which is characterized by a unique mode of communication. These stages fall into three broad phases: coming together, relational maintenance, and coming apart. Although the movement within and between these stages does follow recognizable patterns, the amount and direction of movement are not predetermined. Some relationships move steadily toward termination, whereas

others shift backward and forward as the partners redefine their desires for intimacy and distance.

Other theorists take a dialectal view, arguing that the same series of opposing desires operate throughout the entire span of relationships. These dialectical drives include autonomy versus connection, predictability versus novelty, and openness versus privacy. Since these opposing forces are inevitable, the challenge is to develop strategies for dealing with them that provide relational satisfaction.

Intimacy is a powerful need for most people. Intimacy can be created and expressed in a variety of ways: physically, emotionally, intellectually, and through shared activities. The notion of levels of intimacy has varied according to historical period, culture, and gender. Along with the desire for closeness, a need for distance is equally important. These opposing drives lead to conflicting communication behavior at different stages in people's lives and their relationships. The challenge is to communicate in a way that strikes a balance between intimacy and distance.

Self-disclosure is the process of deliberately revealing significant information about oneself that would not normally be known. The breadth and depth of self-disclosure can be described by the social penetration model. The Johari Window model reveals an individual's open, blind, hidden, and unknown areas. Complete self-disclosure is not common, nor is it always desirable. The chapter listed several guidelines to help determine when it is and is not appropriate. The chapter concluded by describing three widely used alternatives to self-disclosure: lies, equivocation, and hints. It discussed the conditions under which these alternatives can be appropriate.

Key Terms

affinity 170
altruistic lies 191
breadth (of self-disclosure) 185
content messages 169
contextually interpersonal communication 167
control 170
depth (of self-disclosure) 185
developmental model 172
dialectical model (of relational maintenance) 176

dialectical tensions 176
equivocal language 192
immediacy 170
intimacy 180
Johari Window 186
metacommunication 171
qualitatively interpersonal communication 167
relational messages 170
respect 170
self-disclosure 183
social penetration model 185

Activities

1. **Interpersonal Communication: Context and Quality**

   1. Examine your interpersonal relationships in a contextual sense by making two lists. The first should contain all the two-person relationships in which you have participated during the past week. The second should contain all your relationships that have occurred in small-group and public contexts. Are there any important differences that distinguish dyadic interaction from communication with a larger number of people?

   2. Now make a second set of two lists. The first one should describe all of your relationships that are interpersonal in a qualitative sense, and the second should describe all the two-person relation-

ships that are more impersonal. Are you satisfied with the number of qualitatively interpersonal relationships you have identified?

   3. Compare the lists you developed in Steps 1 and 2. See what useful information each one contains. What do your conclusions tell you about the difference between contextual and qualitative definitions of interpersonal communication?

2. **Identifying Relational Messages** To complete this exercise, you will need the help of a partner with whom you communicate on an ongoing basis.

   1. Pick three recent exchanges between you and your partner. Although any exchanges will do, the most interesting ones will be those in which you sensed that something significant (positive or negative) was going on that wasn't expressed overtly.

   2. For each exchange, identify both the content and relational messages that you were expressing. Identify relational messages in terms of dimensions such as affinity, respect, immediacy, and/or control.

   3. Explain the concept of relational messages to your partner, and ask him or her to identify the relational messages received from you during the same exchanges. How closely does your partner's perception match your analysis of the relational messages?

   4. Now identify the relational messages you interpreted your partner as sending during the three exchanges.

   5. Ask your partner to describe the relational messages he or she believed were sent to you on these occasions. How closely did your interpretation match your partner's explanation?

   Based on your analysis of these three exchanges, answer the following questions:

   1. What significant kinds of relational messages are exchanged in your relationship?

   2. How accurate are you in decoding your partner's relational messages? How accurate is your partner in decoding your relational messages?

   3. What lessons have you learned from this exercise that can improve the quality of your relationship?

3. **Your I.Q. (Intimacy Quotient)**   Answer the following questions as you think about your relationship with a person important in your life.

   1. What is the level of physical intimacy in your relationship?

   2. What intellectual intimacy do you share?

   3. How emotionally intimate are you? Is your emotional intimacy deeper in some ways than in others?

   4. Has your intimacy level changed over time? If so, in what ways?

   After answering these questions, ask yourself how satisfied you are with the amount of intimacy in this relationship. Identify any changes you would like to occur, and describe the steps you could take to make them happen.

4. **Striking a Balance Between Intimacy and Distance**   Choose an important interpersonal relationship with someone you encounter on a frequent, regular basis. You might choose a friend, family member, or romantic partner.

   For at least a week, chart how your communication with this relational partner reflects your desire for either intimacy or distance. Use a seven-point scale, in which behavior seeking high intimacy receives a 7, whereas behavior seeking to avoid physical, intellectual, and/or emotional contact receives a 1. Use ratings from 2 through 6 to reflect intermediate stages. Record at least one rating per day, making more detailed entries if your desire for intimacy or distance changes during that period.

   After charting your communication, reflect on what the results tell you about your personal desire for intimacy and distance. Consider the following questions:

   1. Which state—intimacy or distance—seemed most desirable for you?

2. To the degree that you seek intimacy, which variety or varieties are most important to you: intellectual, emotional, and/or physical?

3. Was the pattern you charted during this week typical of your communication in this relationship over a longer period of time?

4. Do you seek the same mixture of intimacy and distance in other relationships?

5. Most importantly, are you satisfied with the results you discovered in this exercise? If not, how would you like to change your communication behavior?

5. **Juggling Dialectical Tensions**   Identify one situation in which you are trying to manage dialectical tensions in your life. (Describe which of the dialectical forces described in this chapter are in operation.) Then answer these questions:

   1. Which of the strategies for managing dialectical tensions listed on page 179 do you use?

   2. How effective is the strategy (or strategies) that you have chosen?

   3. Would an alternative strategy be more effective for managing the tensions in this situation?

   4. How might things go differently if you choose the alternative strategy?

6. **Reasons for Disclosing**   Recall recent personal examples of times when you have disclosed personal information for each of the reasons listed in Table 6-1. Explain your answer by describing:

   - the person who was the target of your self-disclosure

   - the information you disclosed

   - your reason(s) for disclosing

   Based on your findings, decide which of the reasons for self-disclosure are most characteristic of your communication. *Note:* In order to protect privacy, this exercise can be conducted in class by having each member submit anonymous entries.

7. **Effective Self-Disclosure**   Choose a self-disclosing message that is important enough for you to consider sharing. Use the guidelines on pages 189–191 to craft the message in a way that maximizes the chances of having it received successfully. Share your message strategy with classmates, and get their opinion of whether it needs refinement.

For Further Exploration

For more resources about communication in interpersonal relationships, see the *Understanding Human Communication* website at www.oup.com/us/uhc10. There you will find a variety of resources: a list of books and articles, links to descriptions of feature films and television shows at the *Now Playing* website, study aids, and a self-test to check your understanding of the material in this chapter.